# THE TASTE OF OUR TIME

*Collection planned and directed by*

ALBERT SKIRA

BIOGRAPHICAL AND CRITICAL STUDY

BY

# GIULIO CARLO ARGAN

*Translated from the Italian by James Emmons*

# BOTTICELLI

SKIRA

# SANDRO BOTTICELLI

★

## BIOGRAPHICAL NOTE
## THE POETICS OF BOTTICELLI

# BIOGRAPHICAL NOTE

BOTTICELLI was born in Florence in 1445. This date is derived from a document of 1447 in which the painter's father Mariano di Vanno Filipepi refers to his son Sandro as being two years old. A cadastral return made out by his father in 1458 states that Sandro is aged thirteen, *"sta allegere ed è malsano"* (going to school and weak in health).

By 1470 he had made his mark as a painter, for in that year he was asked to contribute the allegorical figure of *Fortitude* (now in the Uffizi), one of the seven Virtues commissioned to decorate the Florentine Mercatanzia (guild of the merchants). By 1472 he was a member of the Company of St Luke and employed Filippino Lippi as an apprentice. In 1473 he painted a life-sized *St Sebastian* (now in Berlin) for the church of Santa Maria Maggiore in Florence.

From then on references to Botticelli become more frequent. In 1474 he entered into negotiations for some paintings in the Camposanto at Pisa, but apparently nothing came of this. In 1478 the Florentine government commissioned him to paint effigies of the Pazzi conspirators after they had been hanged on the walls of the town hall. In 1480 he painted the powerful *St Augustine in his Study* on the choir screen of the Ognissanti church. In 1481 appeared the first Florentine edition of Dante's *Divine Comedy* with the commentary of Cristoforo Landino, illustrated with nineteen line-engravings of the *Inferno* made from drawings by Botticelli. In September 1481 he was summoned to Rome by Pope Sixtus IV to take part in decorating the newly built Sistine Chapel.

◄ SCENES FROM THE LIFE OF MOSES, 1481-1482. DETAIL OF JETHRO'S DAUGHTERS. FRESCO, SISTINE CHAPEL, VATICAN.

Returning to Florence late in 1482, he was engaged to do decorations in the audience chamber of the Palazzo Vecchio (town hall). He did mythological frescos in a villa owned by Lorenzo the Magnificent at Spedaletto near Volterra. He supplied designs for a set of cassone panels illustrating Boccaccio's tale of Nastagio degli Onesti. The frescos from the Villa Lemmi, now in the Louvre, date from 1486. The great altarpiece of the *Coronation of the Virgin* for San Marco and the *Annunciation* for Santa Maria Maddalena dei Pazzi date from 1488.

Among various later references, chiefly to works now lost or never carried out, the most significant is a letter of 1496, sent from Rome by Michelangelo to Botticelli with the request that he remit it to Lorenzo di Pierfrancesco de' Medici. This letter is important as showing (1) that the two artists were acquainted and (2) that Botticelli was still in the good graces of the Medici as late as 1496, which would never have been the case had he then openly adhered to the Piagnoni, the pro-Savonarola faction.

There is in fact no sound historical evidence to support the claim that Botticelli was a follower of the friar and his movement. The most that can be said for certain is that Savonarola's preaching and martyrdom deeply affected the painter's religious outlook and the character of his later work. Botticelli's keen personal interest in the political and religious strife that raged in Florence during the last decade of the 15th century is proved by the Fogg *Crucifixion*, in which we see devils being driven from the city, and by the London *Nativity*, which across the top bears an "apocalyptic" inscription in bad Greek referring to the troubles and unrest of Italy in 1500. As for the veiled accusation of heresy mentioned by Vasari, it was founded entirely on an *Assumption of the Virgin* which is now known to be a work by Botticini. Sandro Botticelli died in Florence and was buried in the Ognissanti church on May 17, 1510.

His turn of mind was "amiable and fun-loving," though "extravagant," according to Vasari, who added that with the passing of the years he took to "living carelessly" and, after becoming a disciple of Savonarola, "gave up working and thus at the end found himself old and poor" and on the brink of starvation. But the "dejected old age" described by Vasari is to be interpreted as a critical opinion, not as a biographical notice. For a thoroughgoing classicist like Vasari, the later evolution of Botticelli's art could only appear as a deplorable turning back of the clock, explicable only by the decay of the artist's creative faculties. Afraid to speak his mind and say, in so many words, that the devotional character of the later works impaired their artistic quality, Vasari altered the biographical facts, just as he had done in the case of Fra Angelico. His bias can be summed up in a few words: for having sought to express religious ideas in the forms of natural beauty, Angelico was a saint and his life was a continuous yearning for perfection; for having rejected natural beauty in order to express the anguish of his own religious adjustment, Botticelli was "extravagant" and "indolent."

Today few painters are more popular than Botticelli. But from the day of his death until he was rediscovered in England about 1870 by Dante Gabriel Rossetti, Swinburne, Walter Pater and Ruskin, he was regarded as a distinctly minor artist, quaint but "primitive." The reason is of course that his art was completely overshadowed by that of Leonardo, Raphael and Michelangelo, who tackled the problems of nature and historical and ideological classicism and restated them in entirely new terms, in complete contrast to Botticelli's poetry of painting, lovely and rare, but limited in scope.

THE NATIVITY (DETAIL), 1500. REPRODUCED BY COURTESY OF THE TRUSTEES, NATIONAL GALLERY, LONDON.

# THE POETICS OF BOTTICELLI

Sandro botticelli was born only seven years before Leonardo da Vinci. Yet Botticelli is always regarded as a Quattrocento painter and Leonardo as a Cinquecento painter. And not without reason. Leonardo originated the modern conception of art as an inquiry, an investigation, a personal quest. Inherited and developed by Raphael and Correggio, this ideal of art culminated in Caravaggio, who restated it in rigorously moral terms, opposing his ethic of action to Michelangelo's ethic of contemplation.

It is true of course that Botticelli's aesthetic ideal was also given a deep moral significance in the art of Michelangelo, but Michelangelo's ethic of contemplation was destined in a few years' time to dwindle into the Mannerists' ethic of form; and it was not to be taken up again until several centuries later, by the early Romantics, in that aesthetic of the Sublime which was, above all else, a nostalgic pining for a long-lost ideal and an attempt to clothe the tattered splendors of the past in the solemn garb of eternity.

Leonardo's new aesthetic, which involved a sweeping renewal of values, came at a critical juncture in history when all traditional values were being challenged. This turning point is clearly reflected in the art of his contemporary, Botticelli, who like him had matured in Verrocchio's workshop, undoubtedly the most stimulating art milieu to be found in Italy in the second half of the 15th century.

The antithesis between Leonardo and Botticelli—which by the way prefigures the future contrast between Leonardo and Michelangelo—rested on the impossibility of reconciling the metaphysical function of art with its historical function. It was impossible to give any further development to the systematic unity of art and knowledge which had been affirmed by the great pathfinders of the Renaissance and which had reached its culmination in the art of Piero della Francesca.

The fact is of course that on the political and religious planes a great future lay in store for this syncretism of art and knowledge, once it had been incorporated in the humanist program gradually drawn up and put into effect by the Church after the healing of the Great Schism (1378-1417), because that program at last supplied historical justification for the Christian faith by embracing Antiquity as its own and proudly pointing to it as the natural philosophy of man, the providential prelude to Christ's revelation of the absolute truth.

But this grandiose, systematic synthesis of history, nature and faith, which was to form the ideological basis of Raphael's classicism, presupposed political conditions very different from those which actually materialized at Florence in the time of Lorenzo the Magnificent. It is obviously possible to give a political interpretation to the soul-struggles of Michelangelo which came so dramatically to a head in the early years of the Cinquecento, and to read into them an ideological contrast between Rome and Florence. But the first signs of this contrast can be discerned several decades earlier in Botticelli's brief, unsuccessful stay in Rome and in Leonardo's undeniable failure at the Vatican.

Botticelli had gone to Rome with political and religious ideals of his own, clearly expressed in his Sistine frescos, which however had no lasting effect on the artistic and religious policies of the Church. But from that time on his painting evolved like a dialectical argument worked out under the unrelaxing, reciprocal tension of religious and artistic problems —the same dialectics, the same tension we find in Savonarola's sermons, to which Botticelli was anything but indifferent. As for Leonardo, he worked on far from Florence and Rome in an atmosphere in which politics involved no particular spiritual problems; not only did he fail to feel any of that reciprocal tension between politics and faith, but he steadily moved towards an undisguised skepticism in political and religious matters and laid down the principle of the absolute autonomy of art and science—the declaration of independence of art and science with respect to religion and politics.

As already intimated, the operative value which in the work of Botticelli and in that of Leonardo led to an open break and precipitated the crisis was neither a religious, metaphysical, political nor historical value, but the union of all these factors in an integrated system. It is an acknowledged fact that Leonardo was the first to wean art from the classical ideal, the first to rebel against the imitation of ancient models. When at the end of the 16th century Caravaggio brutally declared his contempt of the antique, he did no more than add moral emphasis to the indifference shown by Leonardo. What Leonardo contested was not the intrinsic value of ancient art, but the advisability of setting it up as an absolute value, the guiding principle of art creation. The actuality of art, which he sought in the immediate expression of personal feelings, is also bound up with history, but it is based on critical inquiry and insight, not on the blind acceptance of historical values, on the living interests of the present, not on the veneration of the past. His was the intelligent layman's critical examination of history, as against the early humanists' unquestioning faith in history, and once antiquity had come to be judged on its own merits, even when that judgment was tempered by admiration, it had lost its statutory power as an authoritative principle. For Botticelli antiquity had assumed a purely ideal value; it was an ultimate perfection never again to be attained, a remote resort of regrets and desires. For this reason it was neither teachable nor demonstrable; it could neither serve as a tangible example nor bring any influence to bear on the present. Antiquity was no longer "history," i.e. the forging ground of human experience; it lay beyond the range of experience, beyond the mere identifying of it with extant monuments and texts. Antiquity, in a word, had become a sort of metaphysic, a lay religion, a myth. Then it was discovered, with amazement and admiration of the ways of God, that reminiscences of the classical myths had been handed down in the dogmas and written records of Christianity, that in Christ Apollo and Orpheus lived again, and in the Virgin Diana, Minerva and—why not?—even Venus. In this way, for a time at least, the contradictions of history and faith were dodged, as was the moral obligation of distinguishing between truth and falsehood.

Probably never more than in the last years of the 15th century have men so passionately investigated the facts of history or so lovingly pored over the vestiges of the antique. But for neo-Platonists like Poliziano and Marsilio Ficino, as for Botticelli, history was only a prefiguration of contemporary facts and persons, an archetype forever renewed in the present, a cohesive set of symbols. Thus it became a philosophy, but an unsystematized philosophy wholly made up of abstract concepts. As for Christianity, the neo-Platonists conceived of it as an eternal doctrine existing even before the advent of historical Christianity. And for them the very fact that history renewed itself in the present proved that future prospects were illusory, and relations of cause and effect between yesterday and today fallacious. Lorenzo the Magnificent would not have written *"di doman non è certezza"* (no certainty of the morrow) had he still believed in history as a means of stealing a march on the future by meditating on the experience of the past, of overcoming death by leaving to the world the memorial example of great deeds accomplished. On the contrary, Lorenzo keenly felt that only death holds its own and endures (*"solo sta ferma e sempre dura*

*Morte"*), that not history, which is life, but death alone is "master of all and everything." Therefore human actions, devoid of any cause in the past and any durable effect in the future, have no historical value and leave no trace in the swift stream of time, which utterly swamps them.

A facile, skeptical philosophy? Not so much a philosophy as a way of reacting to the misfortunes that were robbing Florence of her place as a hub of history-making events. The very policy pursued by Lorenzo reflects the critical juncture reached by history—and therefore by human actions—as a conceptual value. As a statesman, Lorenzo was shrewd rather than great; an astute diplomat and judge of men, he effortlessly mastered the craft of government and his insight and adroitness saw him through the most difficult situations with unruffled tact and elegance. But with Lorenzo a political action was never dictated by moral considerations or the consequences it might produce; all that mattered were its beauty of form and the perfection with which it was carried out. This, remember, was an age of appearances and fictions, an age in which courage and demeanor were put to the test in tournaments, not in battles, and the social virtues in feasts and pageantry, not in the management of family and state. No wonder that Lorenzo, so avid of glory, cared so little about earning it through brilliant political exploits, but sought it in literature and the patronage of the arts. Art being independent of human actions and lying as it were outside the pale of time, he held it to be the only road to glory and immortality.

This view is implicit in Botticelli's work and in that of all the artists and literati of the Medici court. Art for them is opposed to action, as the eternal is opposed to the contingent, as the infinity of non-time and non-space is opposed to the limitations of time and space. So that not only the idea of history and action was being challenged, but also that of nature, which is time and space. The great men of the early Renaissance had attempted to define nature's laws and bind them into the logic of a system; history, they held, was the logical projection of time, just as perspective was the logical projection of space. But what meaning can nature have if we cease to conceive of her as the product of an initial action accomplished by God the creator, and if we regard reality as continuous movement and change, and God himself as remote and inaccessible, a pure spirit whose infinity meets no limits, not even in the perfection of its own creation?

From then on the great medieval systems of knowledge lost their hold on men's minds, and Leonardo, one of the first to break free, promptly raised the question of experimental knowledge methodically acquired, unhampered by a preconceived system. Botticelli, however, merely concluded that knowledge is useless and impossible. Art dispenses both with knowledge and action, or rather it constitutes the new value arising out of the decline of knowledge and action as operative values. Nevertheless it glorifies nature because she delights the eye with her brilliant variety of forms and colors. Nature is the image of life but not life itself; its bright façades are only so many parti-colored veils floating over an abysmal void, and since they are in a state of continuous flux, there is no way of fastening them down, getting behind them or plumbing their depths. What had happened in connection with moral actions and history, now also happened in connection with nature: just as the great figures of antiquity had turned into symbols and the moral virtues assumed allegorical forms, so the aspects of nature were drained of the substance of truth, dwindled into allusive images and were judged in terms of their beauty alone. The same can rightfully be said of philosophical thought. Marsilio Ficino and Pico della Mirandola set themselves up as philosophers in emulation of Plato and Aristotle. But they were not philosophers; the "fragile scaffolding of concepts" had broken down and their thinking went no further than abstract ideals of "poetry, beauty and love" (E. Garin, *L'Umanesimo Italiano*, Bari 1952, p. 130). Ideas were transformed into religious ideals, while religion in turn was merged into myth, magic and astrology. The technique of argumentation was perfect, but the thought behind it was incapable of defining a conception of the world. Indeed the very facility with which system after system was built up proved that no one any longer believed in them and that the only end in view was a flawless coherence, an ideal perfection, a beauty of thought betokening beauty of soul.

Botticelli's painting in its turn marked a crisis in the evolution of the great art systems built up in the first half of the 15th century. The conception of space and perspective, the conception of form as knowledge or representation of nature, the notion of history as the dramatic figuration of human actions, the role of ethics and religion in art, the status of the artist as a member of the craftsmen's guilds—all this was being challenged and re-examined in the light of that aspiration towards the "beautiful" which was now deflecting the course of art, just as it had deflected the trend of philosophic thought, colored the humanist study of antiquity and influenced moral standards. The result was that in art, as in other fields, what counted was not so much the actual achievement as the specific pursuit of the beautiful.

But what is the "beautiful"? It is what remains of action once it has been dissociated from a moral purpose; what remains of philosophy once it has renounced the constructive virtues of the great systems; what remains of history once it has lost its value as a lesson and example; what remains of art once it has ceased to command belief in its ethical and cognitive content. It is therefore a negative value, the value of a semblance to which no substance or content any longer corresponds. It is, properly speaking, "vanity," a term which, while it might suitably define the enlightened Epicureanism of the cultured Medici court, was shortly to acquire the terrible force of a whiplash as Savonarola used it in his sermons, over and over again, to stigmatize men's vices and frivolity, prophesying the imminent collapse of contemporary society.

Thus for the first time in the history of the Renaissance a painter took as his exclusive aim the quest of the beautiful. There is no denying, however, that by proposing to embody a purely aesthetic ideal in his art, Botticelli reverted in a sense to a medieval, late Gothic outlook, but with a difference: his ideal of *pulchritudo* was not bound up with the Thomist notions of beauty and harmony as tangible signs of the perfection of the Creator, so that his painting, though it is deeply imbued with religious feeling, may only be said to express indeterminate religious aspirations, unconfined to any particular sect or dogma.

Masaccio, Donatello and Brunelleschi had reacted sharply to the medieval identification of art with beauty and chosen to identify art with truth. Then Alberti asserted that the domain of the painter coincided exactly with the domain of the visible world. This identification of art with truth had as its logical corollary the identification of art with form, inasmuch as art forms must always stem from the configurations of reality, from things plainly visible which the eye perceives in their entirety, unambiguously. That is why perspective, which defines forms in space and therefore coincides with the supreme form of nature, is form *par excellence*, the *a priori* form on which all varieties of form depend. And that is why Piero della Francesca, while tending to reduce all forms to their geometrical basis, nevertheless deliberately saturated forms with color and brought them before the eye in all their plenitude.

Can we say as much of Botticelli's painting? His is a painting made up essentially of linear rhythms; but though the eye readily perceives these rhythms, it serves merely as an intermediary, transmitting them to the innermost recesses of our being where they summon up an emotional response. These rhythms, furthermore, set up a movement within the picture itself, inducing as it were a continual give-and-take which prevents the image from "setting" or "crystallizing" into a well-defined form; sudden pauses, shifts, swellings and flashbacks of the line itself prevent the rhythm from lapsing into fixity or taking shape as a form in its own right.

The challenge to form brought with it a challenge to content. Or, more precisely, failing a balance between form and content, the latter immediately came forward as form *in posse*, whether in the case of traditional themes taken in their most literal sense and elaborated on by purely stylistic means, or of allegorical themes which at once substitute one or more images for the original idea. In either case the subject appears as a "beautiful" subject, containing *in nuce* the successive stylistic developments through which it will pass, so that throughout the unbroken evolution from the poetic quality of the theme to the poetic quality of the image no phase of objectivization can possibly enter in, i.e. there can be neither imitation nor contemplation of nature or of an historical example. Botticelli's conception of the "beautiful" then is clearly to be distinguished from the "beautiful" in nature or classical art.

When we read the contemporary Italian poets, we come across the adjective *"bello,"* beautiful, at almost every page: *la bella donna, il bel volto, la bella mano* and so forth. There is little difficulty in ascertaining the qualities embraced by that word; the context of the poem itself frequently suggests that the "beautiful face" is rosy complexioned and pleasingly plump; that the "beautiful hand" is long and white. But the important point is that this adjective serves to bring to mind certain qualities that are not explicitly described; in substance it tells us only that this face and this hand are not an ordinary face and hand, but rank high in the hierarchy of faces and hands and indeed approach an ideal of perfection. Never with Botticelli, as so often in the paintings of Masaccio and Uccello, will a face or hand be distended in perspective or distorted to such an extent that it is either twisted out of recognition or reduced to a mere plastic or spatial element. In a picture by Botticelli we always recognize not only faces and hands, but the very flowers of the fields and the trees of the setting; objects are never twisted or distorted because in themselves they are never considered as factors of a pictorial problem, but simply undergo a process of idealization and selection. But of course the qualification of "beautiful" is not an inherent but an attributed quality; it is like the lover's description of the beloved object. In this sense the notion of the "beautiful" obviously owes much to the neo-Platonic theory of love which, in the late 15th century, borrowed more than one idea from the *dolce stil novo* and from Petrarch. Presupposing in the lover a depth and intensity of emotion of which only the noble heart is capable, the theme of love necessarily gave rise to a language of initiates, comprehensible only to those who truly love.

Let us now seek to determine how and to what extent Botticelli's painting gave concrete form to the poetic ideal in favor with the intellectual élite of the Medici court. As we have noted, Botticelli's creative process involved not a transposition but a transfiguration or sublimation of the object, which therefore remains, qua object, an uneliminable component of the work of art. Taken as a whole, Botticelli's painting offers so extensive a repertory of "objects" that we may well ask ourselves where this assembly of persons and things comes from. Certainly not from the direct observation of the real world.

This way of gathering material, which is common practice with modern painters, was unusual with Quattrocento painters because, for one thing, Quattrocento painting already stood in possession of an "objective" method of recording data, and that method was perspective, whose resultant was form—precisely the value that was being decisively challenged in Botticelli's painting.

It should be borne in mind that Piero della Francesca, supreme theorist of form, lived on to the last decade of the century, and that one of Uccello's most rigorous expositions of perspective—his *Story of the Jew and the Host*—was painted in the very years in which Botticelli completed his training. Now Botticelli's painting is a deliberate, systematic campaign against perspective. Not that he was ignorant of perspective or even violated its laws, on the contrary; but he never used it as the constructive principle of his vision. Take for example a work of his maturity, the *Derelitta*. The vaulted passageway and the steps are shown in flawless perspective, but instead of situating and defining the figure within the setting, this clean-cut perspective isolates and ousts it. What mattered to Botticelli was to convey the impenetrability of that stone wall, the futility of that empty passageway barricaded by the closed door, the unrelieved solitude of the figure. No one knows exactly what the picture was meant to signify. One of the most recent and most plausible interpretations (R. Piccoli, *The Burlington Magazine*, 1930) is that it represents *Veritas derelicta* or *Virtus* severed from *Sapientia* (a theme of topical significance for the intellectuals of that day). Which is to say that the picture symbolizes Man severed from Nature, uprooted and exiled from space, alone with his anguish. Similarly, in the *Birth of Venus*, waves and strand recede into the distance, while the figure looms up naked and alone—doubly naked and alone by its sheer beauty, which transcends the beauty of earthly things.

But the mere isolation of the object in contradistinction to the surrounding space is not sufficient to explain the new, ambivalent significance assumed by the object. This isolating process, a movement in fundamental opposition to perspective, only took shape clearly somewhat later in the art of Albrecht Dürer; and even then its justification was so closely bound up with the Neo-Platonism of Marsilio Ficino that there is no denying the strange kinship between the *Derelitta* and *Melencolia I*. Botticelli of course could not foresee what to Dürer had become clear: the irreducible contradiction between the unity and totality of space, on the one hand, and, on the other, the singularity of the object. The fact that his perspective, like Dürer's, is as flawless as it is pointless, that it is like the surviving superstructure of a demolished space, proves rather that space too has been reduced to the status of an object; it has retained merely an apparent value, it is the symbol but not the representation of reality.

At this point it is important to remember that, from the mid-15th century on, the increasing influx of Flemish paintings into Florence made it imperative to resolve the problem we have touched on: whether or not it was legitimate to consider the constructive application of perspective as the sole method of recording data objectively. It had to be acknowledged that the Flemish way of seeing, operating independently of the laws of perspective projection, allowed of quite as accurate an appraisal, if not an even more accurate appraisal, of the qualities of objects. There can be no doubt, furthermore—as is proved by recurring points of reference—that Botticelli was among the first to note the antagonism between the Tuscan way of seeing, based on perspective, and the Flemish way of seeing, independent of perspective. He was in fact one of the first to realize that that antagonism went deeper than the mere question of optics and rested on the antithesis between the painting of things and the painting of ideas. For anyone considering the problem of space vs. object from a strictly cognitive viewpoint, this antagonism might be resolved by dialectical methods, but such a solution must inevitably lead to a new conception of space; this was the line of research followed by Leonardo. Botticelli however preferred to reason in purely abstract terms: space, being devoid of substance, is merely an image or a symbol; but the object too, being devoid of concreteness, is merely an image or a symbol; therefore between space and object no logical relation can exist, not even a logical antagonism. Neither the one nor the other possesses any effective substance or any certified reality; they are only images, which is to say mere names or words. This reduction of vision and form to what might be called the visual equivalent of words is precisely the quality which, definitively separating Botticelli's painting from the cognitive positivity of the great Quattrocento tradition, assimilated it even structurally to "poetry."

Its name is the most labile, unsubstantial and incorporeal aspect of an object; it is also the only aspect of it which eludes definition in time and space. Having demonstrated the non-spatial character of Botticelli's painting, our next step is to confute every possible interpretation of linear rhythm—the salient feature of his painting—as pure temporality opposed to the spatiality of Piero della Francesca's use of proportions. In a culture as ramified and complex as that of the Italian Renaissance, a culture literally steeped in the study of history, men could not help feeling the need to define time values with the same precision and clarity with which, by means of perspective, space values had been defined. But the artist who raised this problem, by setting up a conception of line based on the Aristotelian *logos* against the Tuscan conception of line based on the Platonic *idea* (in other words, the notion of history as a developing concatenation of events against the notion of history as a static

23

*exemplum*), was not Botticelli; that artist was Mantegna. The rhythm of Botticelli's line has neither continuity nor sequence; it rises and falls, it twists and turns, it falters, resumes it course, leaps forward and splinters off. There is no foreseeing what that line will do. It defines time or duration no more than it defines space. It deliberately ignores or contradicts that sequence of causes and effects which is to time what perspective and scale are to space. In his pictures the narrative itself (if we may speak of narrative in the case of Botticelli) proceeds by impromptu spurts and shifts of movements, followed by long pauses or gaps. It is useless to look to Botticelli for orderly narrative sequence, for a leading dramatic event on which secondary episodes hinge; in fact it is not unusual to find in his arrangement of narrative the same correspondences and repetitions that characterize medieval art.

Turn to the so-called *Primavera*, an obviously allegorical composition which strikes a sharp contrast with the dramatic structure characteristic of historical compositions. Examining the flower-carpeted clearing in the foreground, a botanist could easily recognize and name, one by one, the different herbs and flowers growing there, even though each may have been intended to convey a particular symbolic, magical or astrological meaning. Though these flowers are delineated with painstaking accuracy, they are not lingered over with that keen analytical interest which we feel in Dürer's and Leonardo's drawings. It is as if they had been culled from the pages of a herbal; no sooner have they blossomed than they wither; even their colors —which have never known the splendors of light, which are fragile and delicate, as if miraculously preserved from blight— transmit not the flame of life *in esse* but the waning glow of life that has burnt itself out. Rather than described, these flowers are called by name, and the name of each at once evokes an image which the artist's mind lovingly strives to particularize and define, until finally that image has been substituted for the real object. It is precisely because they have been detached from reality and deprived of corporeal substance that these flowers are "beautiful," beauty being, according to Ficino, *"aliquid incorporeum."* In other words beauty is nothing else but a departure from physical reality, a mysterious transference of things into images.

The image is no less intellectual than form. It is, to be sure, an appearance without substance, but not an appearance consciously dissociated from substance and accepted as a mere datum or sense impression. No painting of the 15th century is so completely detached from sensory experience as that of Botticelli, who nevertheless had behind him a long tradition in which painters' eyes were focused exclusively on the spatial substance of things. But after all, the image, the "beautiful" image, is what remains after that substance has been consumed—an abstract, sublimated residuum transposed on to a plane of pure spirituality where no distinctions or fine shades are any longer possible, where all values are balanced out and merged. Even human actions, once they are represented, lose their actuality; they are lifted from space and time, yet they retain an impress or recollection of the real world from which, not without misgivings, they have been detached.

That the process of transposing the object into the image involves an artifice, that it is not a "natural" but an intellectual process, is obvious; this also holds good for a large part of the "cultivated" poetry of the 15th century. But his being a specifically pictorial problem, Botticelli went straight to pictorial sources in search of his solutions, to Alberti's treatise on painting to start with, for he was aware of the extremely important part it had played in the evolution of Florentine painting. Now Alberti's treatise successively develops two themes: it sets forth Brunelleschi's theory of the architectonic structure of space, which it embodies in a theory of vision; then it seeks to reconcile that theory with humanist literature, which admittedly had little to do with the art of the great pioneers of Renaissance painting and merely insisted on the fact that the new art sank its roots into the antique. Botticelli concerned himself mainly with the second theme of Alberti's treatise, with its specifically humanist and literary side, even going so far as to abide by Alberti's injunctions regarding composition and method. Thus he proceeded from the particular to the whole and set "its every part in movement," taking care to lend *"venustà e gratia"*—charm and grace—to movements and invariably preferring upward movements; he avoided both the crowding and the isolation of figures; he draped garments and wreathed locks of hair according to the precepts laid down in the treatise, and it is certainly not by chance that his *Calumny* is the reconstitution of a classical theme recommended by Alberti.

But while with Alberti the two aspects of the treatise point to a dual interest, in form as the resultant of vision and in images as the heritage of ancient culture, with Botticelli, on the other hand, the predominant interest is in the image. Just as the late Quattrocento humanists looked to the ancient texts rather for the "poetry" and beauty of the discourse than for the moral lesson or the historical testimony contained in it, so with Botticelli the cult of the image constituted one of the key factors in the steadily developing intimacy between painting and poetry. The reason for this is not far to seek: for Botticelli painting tended towards the poetic not simply because of its lyrical nature or by analogy with written poetry, but rather as a vehicle of knowledge—knowledge of nature or knowledge of humanity (i.e. history).

Today no one balks at identifying art with poetry, but at that time the idea came as a complete novelty. Still it made an immediate appeal and even Leonardo, despite his consuming scientific interests, could not help being influenced by it. And if in the end he declared painting to be superior to poetry because it more closely approached to truth, the reason was that he conceived of painting as possessing in the highest degree all those qualities which he felt were lacking in Botticelli's art. But even Leonardo rejected the notion of form as defining a given position in space, and his view of perspective was the very antithesis of that formulated, for example, in Piero della Francesca's treatise on the subject. Leonardo used his mysterious *sfumato* to build up forms to which no bounds can be fixed, forms which expand into outer space until they seem to be physically identified with that space, whereas Botticelli simply opposed the notion of the image, equally valid in painting and poetry, to the notion of form, peculiar to painting. Form is unique and constant, it is a general quality that manifests itself in the particular; images are manifold, innumerable, polyvalent, and pass from one to the other in continual transmutation. Form possesses its own structure and has an unchanging content (nature), which the image does not possess; form is always clear, the image always obscure, allegorical, full of hidden meanings, and in fact neo-Platonic doctrine placed it under the sign of Hermes, god of transmutations, enigmas and allegories (cf. A. Chastel, *Marsile Ficin et l'Art*, Geneva-Lille, 1954, p. 136 ff.).

Gombrich, in a notable article to which we shall refer again, has pointed out that the central figure of the *Primavera* derives, iconographically, from the Virgin in an *Annunciation* by Baldovinetti, and that the *Birth of Venus* is patterned on the traditional lay-out of the Baptism of Christ; he has reconstituted this process of transmutation or *contaminatio* of a sacred theme, which was undoubtedly hastened by the efforts of the humanists to fix a point of convergence between the doctrines of Antiquity and Christianity.

Needless to say, the iconographical resemblance in the two instances just mentioned, far from having any doctrinal significance, was due simply to the poetic content implicit in the image, which is always, by its very nature, ambiguous and polyvalent. Neo-Platonic doctrine aimed at reconstituting with absolute precision the image of the classical divinities; it proposed nothing less than the rehabilitation of classical mythology. But to each of these divinities, in addition to its stock mythological significance, it proceeded to attribute an astrological significance, a moral significance, and so forth. The image, typologically speaking, is constant; but it can assume different meanings and lend itself to different interpretations. As in medieval painting, the use of archetypes (of the human figure, in the case of Botticelli) calls for great skill and refinement on the artist's part if he is to represent them with any originality. He must be able to make us feel that his model is both old and new, both ancient and contemporary; that it belongs at the same time to the world of visual reality and to the world of ideas; that it is both itself and another, many others. Hence the discontinuous rhythm of Botticelli's line: first it suggests a continuity of movement that denies the figures any stable position in space, then it breaks off so repeatedly and abruptly that it reverses our initial impression and even creates a doubt in our mind as to the material existence of the image.

His colors behave in similar fashion: vivid at the outset, they seem to fade and die out on the picture surface without picking up a single ray or vibration of light. It is not unusual for his color to convey symbolic meanings, while the light materializes in gleaming particles which almost literally render the poetic metaphor of "golden sunshine." But because the image is incorporeal, its beauty is indefinable; it is never the beauty of things in themselves, but the beauty which those things transmit or reflect. The image, moreover, is always composite, made up of many images co-ordinated or super-imposed. In the *Primavera*, which may be regarded as a virtually complete exposition of Botticelli's poetics, the Three Graces lightly dancing, with diaphanous veils floating over their bodies, are neither nude nor clothed; it is impossible to say whether the movement of the figures is defined by the bodies or the veils, or whether the veils respond to the motion of the dance or the motion of the wind. These are airy figures, clad in the gauze of the atmosphere, just as the figure of Flora, standing beside them, wreathed in flowers, is both woman and garden. Flowers and jewels too are assimilated to each other; not only do they establish a symbolic relationship between persons and nature, but they show that eyes literally glow like gems, that lips are as red as roses, that flesh has the translucency of pearls. Their very forms are interchangeable: flowers become jewels, locks of hair become necklaces, and so forth.

If the "beautiful" is to be defined as *"aliquid incorporeum,"* as a condition of election to be aspired to and even approached, but never reached or realized, then art cannot be the representation of the beautiful. Granting that all things aspire to a state of perfection and that art is the activated process of that sublimation, Botticelli's poetic practice is seen to have—strange as this may at first appear—much in common with that of Fra Angelico, both alike implying a religious attitude. It is a great mistake to think that Botticelli's art suddenly took a religious turn at a particular point in his career. Admittedly after Savonarola's martyrdom, as the result of an acute mental crisis for which we have actual historical proof, Botticelli's religious outlook took on new poetic and moral depths. But even his early works, usually regarded as profane, not to say pagan, are efforts to link up the Christian myth with the myth of antiquity, while his last works are a frank reversion to the religious tradition of medieval painting.

It is true that Angelico's very positive religious outlook differs greatly from that of Botticelli. In fact it is not too much to say that the secularization of Angelico's monastic poetry, a process initiated by Filippo Lippi and Benozzo Gozzoli, was completed by Botticelli, with the passage from a Thomist aesthetic to a neo-Platonic aesthetic. As a Thomist, Angelico always worked on the basis of a rational premise; that is, with the certitude of being able to represent the Creator through the creature, whose real existence is beyond question. His religious aesthetic, then, by no means ruled out the thesis of art considered as a means of knowledge (which explains the importance of Fra Angelico in the formation of Piero della Francesca). For Botticelli, on the other hand, the problem of art considered as knowledge had been settled for good. For him the "beautiful" is independent of nature; it is not nature that lends her beauty to art, but art that lends beauty to nature, since it is art, or rather artifice, which enables us to elicit the hidden meaning of natural things. Thus Botticelli's attitude is distinctly voluntaristic. Art, he held, is not the representation of the "beautiful" for the good reason that the "beautiful" has no forms to be represented, but only exists as the will to beauty. A whole new aesthetic therefore arises in conjunction with his art, born of the "act" by which that art is produced, born of the will which indefatigably calls forth that "act." Art of this kind is not a revelation but a rite carried out in the worship of an unknown divinity which can only manifest itself indirectly, in the acts of that almost mystic rite. But it is also inspiration or *furor* because the creative act cannot be bent to a pre-established end but takes its rise as a continuous aspiration.

This accounts for the apparently contradictory duality of Botticelli's art, which on the one hand seems to have dipped into the purest poetry and achieved a supreme refinement of form, while on the other it scrupulously adheres to the traditional techniques and procedures of the great craftsmen's guilds—methods with which Pollaiolo, Verrocchio and Leonardo had decisively broken just at that time.

This profound sense of ritual—inseparable from Ficino's neo-Platonic *furor*, which regarded the artist as an initiate and the cult of the beautiful as an Orphic cult—is to be found in every one of Botticelli's works, but most markedly in those which, like the *San Barnaba Altarpiece*, the Berlin *Madonna and Saints* and the Uffizi *Coronation*, were produced in the years 1480-1490 during the acute mental crisis of which mention has just been made. This crisis produced not an overthrow of values, but a phase of clarification which saw the artist redefine his ideological position with redoubled rigor. Rite presupposes myth; and since art is the rite that evokes myth, a world without art would be a world without myths, in other words devoid of images, totally blind; and nature herself, revealed to us only through images and myths, would sink into darkness. Even when he seems most deeply moved by Savonarola's apocalyptic prophesies, Botticelli is unable to imagine a world without myths and images, or without an art that discloses and reveals them. The changing times had completely overthrown the old idea of "vanity": from a positive element in the policy and credo of Lorenzo the Magnificent, it had become a negative element in the fierce crusade of Savonarola.

We can almost see this change taking place when we compare Botticelli's two great "profane" works: the *Primavera* and the *Birth of Venus*. In the first, "vanity" triumphs in the innumerable multiplicity of images, in the continuous, illusive ebb and flow between them, in the profusion of ornament decking and almost concealing the principal image; in the second, the artist embarks on that quest for an essential, "naked" beauty which leads him to abandon the literary artifice of emphatic analogy and to isolate images. In the first we are confronted by an allegory that is still fundamentally naturalistic (not for nothing is it placed under the sign of Mercury), by the transposition of a vague ideal of beauty into the natural appearances which alone, by intimation, can adumbrate that beauty. In the second the allegory is no longer dependent on the mediation of nature; possessed now of all the terseness and simplicity of form peculiar to the symbol, it aims at a direct transposition of the idea into the image. The *Birth of Venus*, then, is the first step towards that pure allegory of ideas, utterly divorced from naturalism of any kind, which reached its climax in the *Calumny of Apelles*, a picture that came almost as a manifesto of the new trend of his art.

But once the myth had been lifted from the framework of nature and could no longer be expressed in terms of natural appearances, then it was free to identify itself with dogma. And rightly so, because the indisputable truth of dogma constituted the one necessary condition needed to give full moral justification to the creative will and to the creative act resulting from that will. It was precisely by virtue of this necessary condition that "vanity" was eliminated from the work of art; and "artistic beauty," nowise identical with "natural beauty" though necessarily modeled on it, could finally be identified with "moral beauty."

Works that seem harsh and remorseful, even bitter, such as the Milan and Munich *Pietàs*, aim in actual fact at being morally beautiful, i.e. at figuring a "beautiful" action as the action that redeems the soul. The tension and sense of tragedy that fill these two pictures stem not from the fiercely realistic treatment of the theme, but from the ceaseless effort to control and dominate the image, which tends to give way to the old allurements, to preen itself in the ornaments of the day, to strike parallels with nature and myth (Christ, for example, is still Apollo or Orpheus or Meleager), to relapse into the prohibited realm of "vanity." It was a struggle between the intellectual image on the one hand and the mythological and natural image on the other; but the result was never in doubt, every trace of naturalism and mythology being finally eliminated from the picture. Michelangelo took up the problem at the very point where Botticelli had left it, but he could do no more than transpose it into the "contraries" of mind and matter, completely sidetracking the problem of nature, which Botticelli had solved to his own satisfaction and which Leonardo restated in entirely new terms.

The consequences of this collapse of the humanist conception of nature as a repertory of names and images to which man must necessarily refer in order to interpret his own spiritual condition, were important and far-reaching. First of all, once naturalistic resemblance had been transformed into an idea and the idea into a dogma, then ornament lost its *raison d'être*; everything that had served to interpret or embellish, to present it "arrayed" as in the Orphic mysteries, now melted into the image, as it were, and combined to define it with absolute clarity, to show it "stark naked." To take an example: the poetic device of entwining and wreathing expressive elements, first applied to the interchangeable images of flowers and jewels in the *Primavera*, was extended directly to architectonic forms in the Berlin *Madonna and Saints*, and then, in the *Last Communion of St Jerome* in New York, was reduced to the interlaced matting, symbol of poverty, that covers the walls and ceiling of the chapel in which the scene takes place. It is true that in certain later works, such as the London *Nativity*, ornament reappears and with it a profusion of ingenuously naturalistic trimmings; yet here, as it so happens, ornament comes as something of a homage or tribute, an act of devout humility testifying that the painter no longer considers himself as an initiate or a knowing intermediary explaining the sacred images. Like Fra Angelico, Botticelli late in life cultivated a seemingly naïve mode of expression and a flow of melodious rhythms which, though simple enough on the surface, are full of impromptu cadences and calculated dissonances; such is the case with the *Miracles of St Zenobius*, manifestly inspired by the predella scenes of Fra Angelico.

From now on, mobilizing every resource of his art, Botticelli threw himself into the struggle against what must have seemed to him to be the evil influence of humanist mythology: the continuous transmutation of images and their meaning, their secret animism, their fickle, pluralistic nature. He meant to hold those images down, to immobilize them, to force them to divulge their innermost being—and thereby to abolish every remnant of profane mythology and confine his images strictly to the realm of sacred myth. The result is, in the Milan and Munich *Pietàs* and even in the London *Nativity*, that groups of figures are welded into a single image, motionless and absolute, yet alive with inner tensions and conflicting forces. This is nowhere more striking than in the Milan *Pietà*, a tight pyramid of figures sealed in a unity that contains its own centers of gravity and lines of force, its own vertices determined by the tragic encounter of two faces, by the repetition of a gesture. This was a new departure in pictorial composition, no longer based on the equilibrium and symmetry of forms but on a synchronizing, contrasting and summing up of expressive accents—a method inimical to space and perspective, which proclaimed the bankruptcy of naturalism and anticipated that composition in terms of inner tensions which we later find in the *Pietàs* of Michelangelo and in Caravaggio's *Entombment*.

Thus it is seen that Botticelli's poetics proved to be not simply a deliberate archaism, but a decisive step towards modern art—not towards that "visionary art" which from Leonardo by way of the Venetians, the Flemings and the Spaniards, led up to Impressionism, but towards that "expressive art" which, through the Germans, gave birth to Expressionism.

WORKS

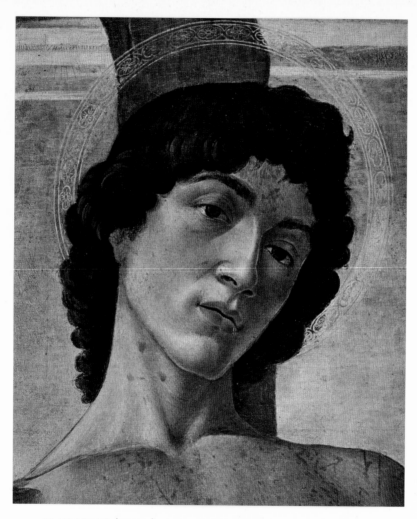

ST SEBASTIAN (DETAIL), 1473. KAISER FRIEDRICH MUSEUM, BERLIN.

# WORKS

Early writers tell us that Botticelli first studied painting with Filippo Lippi and there is no reason to doubt this statement. Still, in his youthful works, modern criticism has detected the influence of Pollaiolo and, above all, Verrocchio; indeed his presence in the latter's studio between 1465 and 1470, side by side with Perugino and Leonardo, is certified by documentary evidence, and the hypothesis that he may have had a hand in the *Baptism of Christ*, traditionally ascribed to Verrocchio with the collaboration of Leonardo, is—though only an hypothesis— quite plausible (cf. C. L. Ragghianti, *Inizio di Leonardo*, in *Critica d'arte*, 1954). On the other hand, Botticelli's style even in his earliest works appears so strongly characterized and pre- supposes so thorough a study of the Florentine tradition that we have no choice but to look deep into the past for the prin- ciples of vision on which he founded his conception of the picture and, in particular, his use of line and color.

Between the premature death of Masaccio (1428) and the start of Botticelli's career, less than forty years had elapsed. Donatello died as late as 1466 and just about that time appeared Uccello's *Story of the Jew and the Host*, the strictest application of perspective to be found in that painter's work. When we remember that one of the fundamentals of Botticelli's art is the rejection of perspective as the structural principle of vision, then his position is seen to be from the very beginning a controversial one. He stood out against the conception of art as knowledge, put forward by the great early Quattrocento masters and solemnly reaffirmed by Piero della Francesca; he stood out too against the art principles represented by Baldovinetti, whose activity spanned nearly the whole second half of the 15th century. Yet, though it is highly original, there is absolutely nothing revolutionary about Botticelli's pictorial language; on the contrary, his is a vocabulary subtly worked out on the basis of those very premises from which, as time passed, he steadily broke away.

In the ten or fifteen years following the death of Masaccio, the leading role in Florentine painting fell to Fra Angelico. In a previous study of that master, we dwelt at some length on the historical importance not only of his painting but of his whole aesthetic founded on the philosophical system of St Thomas Aquinas. Understandably enough, Angelico could never accept a theory that deflected art from its traditional religious function to enlist it in the service of secular knowledge, even though, as a good Thomist, he regarded the knowledge of reality as indirect knowledge of God. So far as he was concerned, perspective was acceptable enough as a reasoning process which, by enabling us to work back from effect to cause, clearly demonstrates the profound rationality of God's creation; but it was not acceptable as the objective structure of reality. An earnest nominalist, he held that God had created all things, together with the light which, emanating from the heavenly bodies, makes those things visible; but space, as the geometric structure of vision, is a concept of the human mind, not a product of the divine creation. Light therefore takes precedence of space; it is an objective reality, the more so as it is lavished upon us by Providence as a means of seeing things, indeed of seeing them in that perfect form in which they were conceived in the creative mind of God and which, through the pall of our sinfulness and sensuality, we perceive as disfigured, tarnished, obscure and heavy. Such were the convictions of Fra Angelico.

The problem of light-form relationship (a reciprocal relation, since light is manifested in form and vice versa) lies at the very basis of that masterpiece by Angelico, the Perugia altarpiece of 1437, which unquestionably influenced Domenico Veneziano and the youthful Piero della Francesca. Both were at work in Florence in 1439, in the church of Sant'Egidio, where they painted a cycle of frescos which no longer exist, but which, to judge by the effect they had on contemporary painting, must have restated in new and ampler terms the problem of the relationship between the effective reality of light and the intellectual reality of space. The evolution of this problem is well known, its successive stages being signalized by the fusion of light and form in Andrea del Castagno's frescos in the church of Sant'Apollonia, Florence; the concord between light and perspective sought for by Domenico Veneziano in the *Santa Lucia Altarpiece*; the whole output of Baldovinetti; and the perfect synthesis of intellectual and intelligible form achieved by Piero della Francesca in his Rimini and Arezzo frescos.

To get an idea of the complexity of the situation at the time, it should be borne in mind that a compromise solution had already been attempted by Filippo Lippi, Botticelli's first master. Lippi was dimly aware of the ideological antagonism between Masaccio and Angelico, Masaccio's ideal being a moral, thoroughly human ideal, while that of Angelico was purely religious. The only common ground between them was provided by nature which, to be sure, embodied the divine message, but which could only transmit it in so far as humanity itself is a part of nature; so that the center of interest tended to concentrate on what is most spontaneous and natural in the human make-up: the emotions.

Taking its rise jointly from the historical naturalism of Masaccio and the religious naturalism of Angelico, Lippi's naturalism embraced a whole field of human experience which Masaccio had rejected as non-historical and Angelico as mundane. The logical consequence of this was twofold: a problem not so much of representation as of visibility was raised, while perspective—for Masaccio the supreme structure of reality, for

Angelico an intellectual or logical instrument—became simply a matter of optics. Thus the position of Ghiberti, who practically reduced perspective to the optical theories of Alhazen and Witelo, is seen to be not an anachronistic survival of medieval notions, but a deliberate, well-justified attempt to reconcile the laws of vision with those of sight.

No wonder then that Lippi looked to sculpture for support; he did so not to reinforce the plasticity of his forms but because sculpture, whose forms actually occupy space and change with the changing incidence of light, goes far more deeply into the problem of visibility than painting does. In sculpture not only is "formal" light also physical light, but the very representation of space is achieved by means of light. With a real depth of hardly more than an inch, a bronze bas-relief must be able to represent the interior of a large building or a landscape of woods and mountains. To get the effect, Ghiberti intensified the play of light, now resorting to gilding, now modeling in oblique planes that facilitate the transmission of light. Donatello on the contrary, for whom perspective was a spatial-temporal condition for the highly dramatic staging of historical narrative, could not make shift with an indefinite spatial system and indefinite light, which would have crippled the dramatic tension. Donatello's "squashed" relief flattens forms down, while Ghiberti rounds them out; the rounded form has no definite contours, while the flattened form is sharply defined by its luminous edge standing out against the cast shadow that separates it from the ground plane. It is this play of light and shadow which, forming the liaison between figure and space, defines movement, action and the dramatic character of the scene. And as the years passed and Donatello's work grew increasingly high-strung and dramatic, he laid increasing stress on the feverish rhythm of his line, while the intensity and vibrancy of light were heightened accordingly.

Now the San Lorenzo pulpits, which mark the peak of Donatello's dramatic poignancy of line expressed in terms of light, were executed just as Botticelli was beginning to meditate on the problems of his art. Nor—in our search for clues to the determining factors in Botticelli's orientation—should we forget that Agostino di Duccio, the most acute and sensitive of Donatello's disciples, was just then working out an exclusively linear interpretation of his master's art, whose dramatic, realistic handling of history he completely eliminated.

If in sculpture it is light that visibly brings line to life, in painting the problem of transposing light values into line values—or, in the last analysis, empirical sensations into intellectual terms—is much more complex. We find the first signs of that transposition in Lippi's Tarquinia *Madonna*, painted in 1437. Here, as in Donatello's flattened reliefs, light is internal, coming from within the space with which it is identified; it models forms and mixes with colors. Space is no longer homogeneous but partitioned off according to the "natural" movements and variations of light; and line now defines not the contours of objects but planes and zones of light. Lippi's Tarquinia *Madonna* and Fra Angelico's Perugia altarpiece were painted in the same year; they represent opposite extremes in a debate over the quality—celestial or natural—of light.

Fra Angelico fanned the quarrel to a flame when, in the frescos painted in the convent cells at San Marco, he reaffirmed his religious stand with a dogmatic rigor easily accounted for by the fact that these paintings are not intended for the eyes or minds of men who continue to stumble towards salvation through the pitfalls of worldly experience, but for monks, for ascetics. For men who have embraced the monastic rule, there is no point in showing nature as a path to salvation; light, for them, means the light of revelation or dogma, an absolute light that cannot possibly mingle with natural objects. These in fact are reduced to bodiless images, to symbols, while light, no longer possessed of natural substance, no longer issuing from natural sources, is intelligible rather than visible. How completely this rigorously ascetic or theological painting ruled out every problem of space may be seen by comparing it with that of Uccello, who shut himself up in a closed, "totalitarian" world ruled by perspective alone, where he proposed to define objects not by light but solely by their position in space. In so doing, he went so far as to alter natural colors and use tones exclusively as a means of distinguishing the different perspective planes.

We have until now purposely deferred discussion of the painter—Andrea del Castagno—who more than any other strove to reconcile Masaccio's plasticity with Angelico's luminosity, and to combine them into a single aesthetic of line taken in the strict sense of "drawing." Castagno had the stature of the great humanists, and the problem that engrossed him was a human problem, not one of nature. The initial terms of that problem lay in the moral grandeur of Masaccio's human sympathies and in the dramatic, energetic humanism of Donatello's keen sense of history. But the heart of the question was no longer the fundamentally ethical or fundamentally historical nature of mankind, but the earthly destiny of mankind. Castagno thus brought into play the theme of individual, voluntary action —action not necessarily dramatic however, because it takes no account of external contrasts; it stands or falls solely on the strength of the volitional impulse inspiring it. This theme wants the strong personality, the hero, and it is the first indication of that irrational, voluntaristic drive which was to dominate Florentine painting throughout the late 15th century, and which, by way of Pollaiolo and Botticelli, culminated in Michelangelo.

There is no difficulty in tracing Castagno's heroic ideal back to the humanist philosophy of Coluccio Salutati and, more particularly, Leonardo Bruni; of the latter in fact, who died in 1444, Castagno painted a posthumous portrait. The *terribilità* of his figures manifestly reflects Bruni's ideas on the ethical superiority of the active life over the contemplative life, of Mary over Martha, of the great captains over the great philosophers. His series of *Famous Men* is conclusive proof of this. But that will to action which makes for greatness in a man and gives him a worthy place in history also separates him from nature or, more precisely, links him up not with the inert objects of reality but with the unseen energies and life-forces of nature. In Castagno's compositions there are seldom any secondary figures, but only protagonists; and they are never shown as participants in nature in a landscape setting; all that remains of nature is her most "spiritual" and active element—light.

In spite of the loss of the frescos he painted in 1451 in Sant'Egidio (the same Florentine church in which Domenico Veneziano and Piero had worked twelve years before), his Sant'Apollonia frescos suffice to show how Castagno conceived the problem of space-light relationship. As an extremist, he had no qualms about accepting the theological conception of light as revelation, exemplified by Fra Angelico in the San Marco frescos. Thus his heroes, "absolute," voluntaristic and irrational in their actions, are much more closely in touch with the universal, with God, than with nature and their fellow men. His light, indeed, is a dry white light, devoid of substance, all-pervading. It is not to be stopped or screened by the solid, opaque masses of intervening objects, which it traverses as if they were transparent, yet without depriving them of their consistency and weight. It dissolves the matter that renders them inert, while its own light-energy nevertheless preserves and intensifies the life-force and energy contained in them. For this reason Castagno's light not only does no violence to the notion of space, but actually identifies itself with space; it might be described as perspective light.

This in sum is the problem tackled by Lippi, but transposed now from the empirical to the intellectual plane. As a humanist, Castagno reasoned in terms very similar to those of Alberti; for him the guide lines of perspective projection coincide with the "oblique and centric rays of light." But this solution was not strictly optical inasmuch as figures were freely traversed and built up by light, whose directive rays determined the orientation, inclination and relationship of planes.

Thus to the binomial of light plus perspective a third term was added: anatomy, which formulates the structural principles of the human body just as perspective formulates those of space. The result was the isolation and glorification of the human figure, posited as the supreme synthesis or absolute form of reality (and this conception was powerfully furthered by the humanist ideal of the "statue"). But if the human figure is to stand as the supreme value, then obviously it cannot be treated as a mere object located in space and dependent for definition on the incidence of light; it cannot, in a word, occupy a subordinate position with respect to nature. So the human figure was reduced to the one element which it has in common with space-light and which, like the latter, embodies energy, tension and the principle of movement; that element is line.

In this way line or "drawing" came as the by-product of perspective, its ultimate configuration, not only naturalistic but anthropomorphic. Line of course presupposes the contraries of "matter" and "light," but it overcomes the antinomy between them by positing itself as the absolute expression of the human intellect and will. In this sense drawing can no longer obey the specific visual principles peculiar to the various arts, but necessarily precedes every technical prescription and stands as a principle common to all the arts. It was not by chance that Pollaiolo and Verrocchio, who paid particular attention to problems of line, were painters and sculptors at the same time.

JUDITH WITH THE HEAD OF HOLOFERNES, CA. 1470. ($12\frac{1}{4} \times 9\frac{3}{8}''$)
UFFIZI, FLORENCE.

THE MADONNA OF THE EUCHARIST, CA. 1472. (33 × 24¾″)
THE ISABELLA STEWART GARDNER MUSEUM, BOSTON.

That Botticelli actually worked for a time in Verrocchio's studio, alongside Lorenzo di Credi, Perugino, Botticini and Leonardo, is vouched for by early writers and corroborated, moreover, by the stylistic analysis of such works as are known to date from before 1470, e.g. the *Virgin and Child with Angels* in the Uffizi. At the same time his early works abound in reminiscences of Filippo Lippi, particularly noticeable in the two panels illustrating the story of Judith and Holofernes (Uffizi), datable to about 1470; while in the *Fortitude*, a dated work painted in that very year for the Florentine Mercatanzia, the influence of Pollaiolo is by no means limited to the iconographical analogy with the other figures designed by that master for the same series. The problem of Botticelli's early training is therefore seen to be extremely complex. It was presumably his contact with Lippi that led him to approach painting not from the historical but from the purely human angle of man's emotional response to nature.

But the antithesis between Lippi's tender cult of nature and Castagno's fierce cult of history is not so clean-cut as it seems, for the two great complementary problems—analysis of nature and analysis of man—always tended to coalesce. Pollaiolo was the first to realize that Castagno's strict voluntarism was incompatible with the rationalistic conception of space as perspective and of time as history. Pollaiolo's ideal was not real action but potential action, not will-power directed to a given end but the energy generated by the emotions and the will conjointly. Unconcerned with the historical origins and moral purpose of an action, he went straight to the energizing tension, the *furor*, of an action in the process of being performed. With Pollaiolo the gestures of a figure are dissipated into the landscape and transformed into a tremor that ripples through space to the farthest horizon. He restated the problem of nature not as a static, unchanging reality, but as space engendered and animated by the convulsive movement of human figures; even the light filling that infinite space seems to well up from the movement of the figures, generated in spurts and flashes by vivid accents of line and color. No longer does history precede and condition human action, which, as it has no limits in space, has none in time either and is at once actual and remote; every action is regarded as having occurred in an immemorial past, and as recurring with undiminished intensity before our own eyes. Hence the revival of mythology and allegory that came in the wake of Castagno's obsession with history. Verrocchio went even further: his feeling for nature—whose main ingredients are movement and energy—is inseparable from the energy that goes to make up the specific character of man and his modes of actions. Feeling and will constantly tend to be intellectualized because they contribute in equal measure to the simultaneous and indistinguishable knowledge of the self and the world. Here we reach the point at which the paths of Botticelli and Leonardo diverge.

Botticelli's *Judith* enables us to gauge the deep change that had come over the highly emotional feeling for nature expressed by Lippi in, for example, his choir frescos in Prato Cathedral, a late work. In his fine essay on Botticelli in *The Renaissance*, Walter Pater describes Judith, "returning home across the hill country, when the great deed is done, and the moment of revulsion come," and goes on to characterize Botticelli's art as a blending of his "sympathy for humanity in its uncertain condition" with his "consciousness of the shadow upon it of the great things from which it shrinks." Having killed Holofernes, Judith returns home with his head; it is a return to nature, a return to normal feelings after an "heroic" action which was, nevertheless, an act of violence. The two figures seem to have grown out of the landscape, born of the juxtaposition of zones of light and shadow against the almost uniform luminosity of the background. These juxtaposed zones of light and shadow are interwoven amidst the wavy folds of garments, in a spirited pattern of filaments of light and furrows of transparent shadow. Lines—which are no longer the "surface edges" of Alberti—thus arise from the intensification of "spatial" light, from its subtle contrasts with shadow. But that light and that shadow are not mere sensory notations; their value is an essentially intellectual value, and their contrast is the contrast between an active, spiritual, incorporeal substance (light) and an inert, opaque substance (matter).

In the companion picture of the *Finding of Holofernes' Body*, the luminist origin of line is even more evident. The whole scene is set in a zone of twilight contrasting with the luminous depths of the background, which we glimpse through the half-drawn flaps of the tent. It is worth noting that this arrangement, absolutely new at the time, is substantially the same as that, on a far grander scale, of Leonardo's *Virgin of the Rocks*, painted about twelve years later. To the pool of light in the background corresponds a stream of softer, more diffuse light apparently pouring in from the front, which washes over the body of Holofernes and is gradually attenuated as it penetrates into the picture. The figure of the warrior bending over his dead chieftain and that of the dismayed priest are both defined by light, by interwoven threads of light which recall the golden highlights of miniatures.

But in order to decompose light into purely linear elements, it was first necessary to determine the conditions of tangency between incoming light rays and stationary objects; and these conditions could only be fulfilled by violating that identity or collimation between perspective lines of projection and impinging rays of light which we noted in Andrea del Castagno's work. Thus it was that both the intellectual and optical aspects of the perspective problem were cancelled out.

Let us remember that by this time perspective had ceased to be an entrancing problem and was no longer a novelty even for such men as Baldovinetti and Ghirlandaio. In fact it was Ghirlandaio who reduced perspective to "normal" vision and made it the basis of a prosaic narrative painting, which justified Botticelli's reaction to the opposite extreme of poetic painting, fundamentally opposed to perspective. And his yearning for the poetic, the anti-prosaic, revealed itself straightaway in an unmistakable deviation from normal vision. Proof of this is the Holofernes panel, which is organized by sinuous, oblique lines of projection which prevent a stable positioning of the figures in space and bind them together in foreshortenings that take no account of the laws of perspective. Thus each figure, no longer integrated into a precise framework of perspective, stands on its own by virtue of the action it performs, the part it "speaks," the note of sentiment it expresses. This method of composition proceeds by a sequence which is neither logical nor natural, but which we find throughout the artist's work. It shows that he no longer regarded historical narrative as the reconstitution of a bygone event, but as the poetic, nostalgic evocation of it.

The figure of *Fortitude* is known to date from 1470. The commission for an allegorical series of the seven cardinal and theological Virtues to decorate the Florentine Mercatanzia (guild of the merchants) was given to Piero Pollaiolo, with his brother Antonio as guarantor, in August 1469; in December the first figure, *Charity*, was ready. Apparently the authorities were dissatisfied with the work, since Verrocchio was asked to submit designs and in June 1470 the figure of *Fortitude* was allotted to Botticelli. Naturally the lay-out of the picture was that prescribed for the entire series by Piero Pollaiolo, perhaps on the advice of Antonio who in fact provided a design for *Charity*. But the style shows that at this stage of his development Botticelli had one eye fixed on Verrocchio and the other on Antonio Pollaiolo. He obviously patterned his figure on the seated statuette of John the Baptist on the silver cross executed by Pollaiolo some time after 1457 for the church of San Giovanni. It is interesting to note that the small shrine containing this cross almost exactly reproduces the radial structure of Brunelleschi's lantern atop the dome of Santa Maria del Fiore. From this structure in strict perspective Botticelli took over the projecting volutes and the deep recessing of the archivolt, so that the figure, seated frontally with legs bent in such a way as to emphasize the inordinately long bust, stands out against a perspective background which, however, does not frame it but acts simply as an element of contrast. This architecture then is a background moved radically forward, we might almost say a landscape symbolically translated into architectonic forms; it is stately architecture "sensitized" in every detail through subtly pointed trimmings reminiscent of Verrocchio's plastic ornamentation. In short, without sacrificing the formal elegance of the architecture, Botticelli gave it the variety and mobility of those forms peculiar to natural things. The result is that this architecture acts as a source of light, its sharp angles and clean profiles reflecting a whole play of crisscrossing lights that give forms a crystal-clear hardness and transparency.

When in 1473 he painted a life-sized *St Sebastian* for the church of Santa Maria Maggiore, the "heroic" figure of the martyr saint prompted him to refer to the work of Andrea del Castagno, of which we find distinct traces in the modeling of the face and body by luminous planes, in the diaphanous forms, in the upright, frontal posture of the figure. But again, as in the *Fortitude*, image values prevail over form values, because it is precisely the poetic quality of the image that enables the theme of the hero to be merged into that of the martyr, and the Christian saint to be assimilated to a pagan god.

There is no foreground to the picture, and every perspective connection between the figure, developed vertically, and the distant landscape has been discreetly suppressed. In Pollaiolo's *St Sebastian*, painted about 1475, a foreground is included and peopled with the figures of the executioners; this lends a strong dramatic accent to the scene. Botticelli, however, gives us purely and simply the presentation of an image instead of the representation of a dramatic event. The distant landscape, flooded with light beneath a boundless sky, still retains—perhaps by way of Perugino—a faint flavor of Piero della Francesca's landscapes; on the other hand, the incisive detail of the tiny figures, trees and buildings in the distance betrays his first contact with Flemish painting.

A trained eye will note at once the distinctly anti-perspective structure of that landscape background, entirely built up in oblique, divergent, zigzag lines, which bring the diffuse light of the picture depths to focus on the figure of St Sebastian. The paths of focused light are insistently restated by the arrows piercing the figure. Thus the light, of varied incidence and intensity, strikes a body which cannot be said to stand in a well-defined space, and which, rendered transparent by opposing rays of light, can no longer be called a solid body (in the Albertian sense of a thing "which occupies space"); in the same way, the lines can no longer be called contours (in the Leonardian sense of "limits of bodies").

Even when many figures people the scene, the artist is more concerned with the unity of the image than with the composition of the narrative he is dealing with. It had long been customary to treat the Adoration of the Magi as a pageant or procession, full of worldly color, and Botticelli gladly conformed to this traditional interpretation. Yet, in the London tondo, instead of describing figures one by one, he groups them in a triangular mass pointed deep into the picture, its vertex and vanishing

ST SEBASTIAN, 1473. (76¾ × 29½″)
KAISER FRIEDRICH MUSEUM, BERLIN.

THE ADORATION OF THE MAGI, BEFORE 1475.
(DIAMETER: 51½″) REPRODUCED BY COURTESY OF THE TRUSTEES,
NATIONAL GALLERY, LONDON.

point being formed by the Virgin and Child; and on top of that mass stand the ruins of an ancient edifice, its shining planes and elegant pillars towering up until cut off by the edge of the panel. The patch of landscape on the right, with a leafless tree and a coppice of light-colored treetrunks beneath dark foliage and a distant castle, might have been lifted all of a piece from some Flemish painting. The limpid sky and the smooth, burnished architecture reflect light abundantly on to the figure group, in which, once again, lines are volatilized into threads of light, while the rhythm of movements springs from the multiplicity of light-sources and the complexity of criss-crossing rays. No structural or perspective link connects figures, ruins and landscape. The circular shape of the picture, though it centers the entire composition on the Virgin and Child, does not co-ordinate the different parts, but on the contrary sharply disting-uishes the large figure group, spread over an inclined plane, from the vertical impetus of the architecture and the inward thrust of the landscape. Each of these elements, moreover, has its own ideological justification. To begin with the most obvious allusion, the ruins are a reminder of antiquity, of Rome, of the continuity of ideas linking classicism with Christianity; the allusion is all the more pointed for the fact that the edifice shown here—which looks less like a ruin than like a new building in process of construction—may be construed as symbolizing the revival of classicism in consequence of the very event that heralded a new era and gave birth to a new, milder, more humane society, i.e. the society we see here crowding round the manger. The peacock, as an exotic bird, manifestly signifies that the event occurred in a distant eastern country; at the same time, the presence in the crowd of wise men in oriental costume may allude to the Easterners who had come to Florence for the church council and to the importance of their role in the development of that new neo-Platonic culture of which Botticelli, as is well known, was an enthusiastic adept. As for the late winter landscape barely touched by the fingertips of spring, it too is a transparent allusion to the humanist dream of a *renovatio*; it hints at the rebirth of nature, just as the architecture and the figure group suggest the rebirth of culture, of *humanitas*.

These ideas are reverted to and re-emphasized in the Uffizi *Adoration of the Magi*, painted a few years later, about 1475. The old man kneeling at the Virgin's feet is Cosimo de' Medici, while all the bystanders are courtiers or intimates of the House of Medici (the last figure on the right, looking out of the picture, is a self-portrait of the artist). The personal—not to say political—glorification of Cosimo here being absolutely explicit, the remaining allusions are minimized, and even reduced to purely symbolic referents. The ruined arches of ancient Rome are merely a "stage-prop" in the background; the landscape has been suppressed altogether; the peacock suffices to symbolize the East. The picture being avowedly social and political in intent, the painter makes no attempt to disguise the fact that it is all a fiction, an elaborate dumb-show, and from this time on fiction became the essential ingredient of his poetics. The combination of ruins, rocks and lean-to, sheltering the Holy Family, is patently a stage decor; and in it, as in all stage sets, every element is an integral part of the whole, with an allusion or even a symbol attaching to it. For example, the idea of nature is here expressed by the rough bark of the treetrunks; the idea of poverty by the shaky planks of the lean-to; the idea of ruin and *renovatio* by the flowers and leafy plants that have grown from the chinks of the shattered wall.

The first painter to surround the miraculous vision of a sacred event with an assembly of notables, literati and humanists, almost raising them to the rank of officiants or celebrants of a rite, was Fra Angelico in the San Marco *Descent from the Cross* (ca. 1440), which may be considered as the ideal figuration of

THE ADORATION OF THE MAGI, CA. 1475. (43⅝×52¾″) UFFIZI, FLORENCE.

*docta pietas.* With Angelico, as now with Botticelli, rite evokes myth; but while in Angelico the candid naturalism of the background clearly implies the necessity of setting the sacred miracle in that continuous miracle we call nature, in Botticelli, on the other hand, the undisguised ceremonial and political intent of the picture destroys the "naturalness" of the myth and

the rite. The latter indeed assumes an artificial—or official—
character that the artist makes no attempt to conceal. As a
result, the sacred theme moves back from the foreground to
the vanishing point, nature herself is reduced to a few significant
symbols, and the evocation of the myth is no longer "natural"
but intellectual.

THE ADORATION OF THE MAGI (DETAIL), CA. 1475. UFFIZI, FLORENCE.

Fra Angelico too had had a political thesis to expound: his religious naturalism was motivated by a desire to enlighten the Florentine bourgeoisie, to urge upon it a renewed sense of its religious role as the moral pillar of society. Religious and political aspirations exactly tallied in Fra Angelico's mind. For Botticelli, though always closely connected, they were distinct nevertheless, and his figures are not the celebrants of a rite but simply perform an act of devotion and homage. Botticelli, of course, was committed to the ceremonial, educational function of art no less than Angelico was committed to his mission of religious apostleship. In fact in the second half of the 15th century Botticelli was the foremost exponent of a ceremonial, processional, poetic-social art, as against those painters who identified creative art with the speculations of the thinking mind in its quest for knowledge of reality.

THE ADORATION OF THE MAGI, 1481-1482. (27⅝ × 41″) MELLON COLLECTION, NATIONAL GALLERY OF ART, WASHINGTON, D.C.

But here a further distinction must be made. The earliest convincing demonstration of the possible identity of art and knowledge, indeed of art and science or art and philosophy, had been made by Piero della Francesca. But Florentine painting had been consistently repudiating this identity for some time now, beginning perhaps with Andrea del Castagno and Paolo Uccello, certainly with Antonio Pollaiolo. This being the case, what was it that led Botticelli at this late stage to take so polemical a stand in the matter?

The explanation lies in the fact that in those very years, and in Verrocchio's entourage, another great artist had also taken a firm stand against Piero's cult of form, but not for the same reasons as Botticelli. That artist was Leonardo da Vinci. He of course never attempted to enlist art in the service of knowledge and in fact made a point of drawing the line between art and science; still he maintained the inevitable relationship between art and all the aspects of the visible world, and even consolidated that link by assigning art the task of revealing to us that which, though not immediately visible, is nonetheless real. Thus in his hands art became research and investigation; it was even turned into a quest for a "beauty" assumed to exist, elusive and diffuse, in reality. The contacts between Botticelli and Leonardo were not confined to the period of youthful comradeship in Verrocchio's workshop; for a long time thereafter a kind of reciprocal magnetism alternately repelled and attracted these two personalities—opposite numbers in so many ways yet alike in creative power. Each, studied in retrospect, seems consciously or unconsciously to have defined his position with respect or in contradistinction to the other.

One of the major contrasts between them is clearly brought out in Leonardo's writings. He lays polemical emphasis on the fact that Botticelli scorned to paint landscapes because, as he is supposed to have said, "simply throwing a sponge dipped in colors against a wall leaves a stain in which a fine landscape can be seen." To this sally Leonardo wryly appends his own opinion: that Botticelli "made very feeble landscapes." Now Leonardo left Florence in 1481. When he returned it was only to involve himself in his ideological quarrel with Michelangelo (which in a sense was the logical continuation of his conflict with Botticelli). It is highly improbable that he took any notice of the work then being produced by his former companion, now fast developing into a religious zealot. We are thus entitled to assume that the passage quoted above reflects the youthful experiences of their early period in Florence. No wizardry is needed, moreover, to guess that Botticelli's quip about landscape and a blotch of colors on the wall was not an idle remark, but a "crack" at Leonardo's own way of painting landscape. That, at any rate, is how Leonardo himself interpreted it; he pondered so long and deeply over that criticism of his methods that in the end he built up a whole theory of the spots on walls and the stimulating effect they have on the painter's imagination. As for Botticelli, the works he painted between 1470 and 1480 prove that he possessed in the highest degree the qualities that make a great landscape painter. Leonardo was not the man to overlook such qualities, but what he objected to was Botticelli's way of contriving landscapes intellectually and assigning an ideological or symbolic value to each element separately.

A new and important factor, and matter of great topical interest at the time, was the rise of Flemish painting, equally appreciated by both men but for very different reasons. For Leonardo Flemish painting represented a direct, unbiased vision of reality, a welcome test of empirical methods unemcumbered by hard-and-fast rules of perspective. To Botticelli (who thereby

THE ADORATION OF THE MAGI (DETAIL), 1481-1482. MELLON COLLECTION, ▶
NATIONAL GALLERY OF ART, WASHINGTON, D.C.

anticipated Michelangelo's antithesis between nature and idea) Flemish painting appeared as the representative conversion of art into "nature"—in other words, as the dialectical antithesis and, at the same time, the necessary complement of his own conception of art as *humanitas*, i.e. as culture and civilization.

Without going into the question of Leonardo's work prior to 1480, but simply making allowance for his presence—proved by extant documents—in Verrocchio's workshop, we can safely assert that his approach to painting was, like Botticelli's, determined by the question of line-light relationship. This is largely borne out by his Uffizi *Annunciation* and by that part of Verrocchio's *Baptism of Christ* which is ascribed to his hand. His starting point was therefore very close to that of Botticelli. Endless debates have arisen as to whether Leonardo's outlook was neo-Platonic or Aristotelian. This much is historically certain: though his later development may have been tinged with Aristotelianism, his point of departure was the neo-Platonic culture which, at Florence in the last decades of the 15th century, was the official culture. Indeed his poetic ideal, like that of Botticelli, is a cult of *furor*, i.e. of inspiration, not of contemplation or speculation. But for Botticelli this meant the true Ficinian *furor*, i.e. tension, religious fervor, love, will to transcendence, whereas for Leonardo it was the ardor of experiment, the fever of analysis and research. We have said that Leonardo made a distinction between science, which aspires to truth, and art, which aspires to beauty; here, by positing art as the pursuit of beauty, he stands in substantial agreement with Botticelli. But while the latter never believed in the possibility of positive knowledge, Leonardo ardently believed in it. Thus the "beautiful," which for Botticelli lay beyond reality and experience, was sought for by Leonardo within reality and experience. Identifying oneself with reality and participating in its movements and changes, this was Leonardo's *furor*.

As for the problem of light, both men approached it from the standpoint of neo-Platonic doctrine, which defined light as a scale of values going from "the invisible light of God *(Deus lux summa luminum)* to the darkness of matter, in which light seems to die down to the point of extinction" (E. Garin, *op. cit.* p. 127). Neither man ever seemed to ask himself what the mind's reaction is to the phenomenon of light. Their solutions, while diametrically opposed, agree in that they both sidetrack the dual difficulty of source and screen. Botticelli opted for the "spiritual" solution of transparency or diaphaneity; that is, he denied light any physical substance and refined matter down to that minimal element which, as the supreme expression of the human mind or spirit, can be identified with light: line. Leonardo, for his part, looked to atmosphere as the substance most closely related to light and the vehicle without which light would be motionless, invisible, intransmissible; that is, he resolved the problem by way of opacity or penumbra. Botticelli's solution was purely intellectual; Leonardo's was based on experience.

This contrasting vision is graphically illustrated by a comparison of two portraits painted at roughly the same time, about 1475: Botticelli's *Man with a Medal* and Leonardo's *Ginevra Benci*. What Botticelli wanted to avoid was a solid, opaque figure in space, screening off the light and built up in juxtaposed planes of light and shadow. But he also wanted to avoid having the diaphanous face flooded by a direct—i.e. naturalistic—inrush of light from the background. He therefore isolated the face against the dark screen of the hair. In the background on the left flows a river whose irregular shoreline, in violation of all the laws of perspective, runs parallel to the profile of the face; thanks to this sharp contrast between the dark riverbank and the scintillating waters, the light is shunted into the foreground, glides across the upper folds of the coat and illuminates the face. Even the light ostensibly pouring in from the front,

PORTRAIT OF A MAN WITH A MEDAL, CA. 1475. (22⅜ × 17¼")
UFFIZI, FLORENCE.

caught and reflected by the gold medal, is thrown on to the face by the bold foreshortening of the contracted hands. Complex and skillfully concealed, this play of reflected light—this indirect lighting—inevitably involved the necessity of defining the composition by line. In the background, in the jagged pattern of the rivershore, in the face, in the sensitive contour of the cheek against the dark head of hair, everywhere line marks the limit between two zones of color of differing light intensity. And since light is here ceaselessly generated by the opposition of darker and lighter tones, this work better than any other brings home to us the linear basis on which Botticelli's style arose. It would be absurd to qualify that line as a meaningful incidental or a graphic abstraction; his line is born of the conjunction of light and space, but it is also the intellectual factor which definitively eliminates matter, even that of space and light. The multiplicity and divergence of the directive rays of light resulted in a displacement of axes, an abnormal dislocation of volumes and planes, and an obvious asymmetry of forms—to such an extent that line never quite succeeds in enclosing a form and therefore cannot properly be called a contour or "limit." Hence that continuity of movement or that alternate rupture and resumption of movement which is rhythm, and which is the antithesis of proportion, i.e. of equilibrium or perspective symmetry.

The very opposite is true of Leonardo's *Portrait of Ginevra Benci*, in which the juniper trees (which are also a symbolic allusion to the model's name) act as a screen filtering the light and diffusing it from the landscape background on to the face, whose softly rounded features, smooth contours and attenuated angles facilitate a uniform distribution and even penetration of light. Unlike Botticelli's portrait, which is sinewy and anxious, Leonardo's is so serene and relaxed that it was long attributed to Lorenzo di Credi, though no known work by this painter can stand comparison with it. This portrait proves, however, that Leonardo's fine poetic frenzy, that *furor* of which we have just spoken, was not developed until a few years later, round about 1480, when he had gone more deeply into the question of space-light relationship.

Leonardo's unfinished *Adoration of the Magi* is a typical example of his poetic *furor*. First of all it decisively reverses the compositional scheme of Botticelli's Uffizi *Adoration of the Magi*. In the latter the Virgin and Child are placed at the most distant point of the setting, well above the group of bystanders wreathed around them; Leonardo's Virgin is brought forward into the very center of a turbulent group of figures, who seem to swirl around her as an indistinct mass of light and shadow. The ruins melt into the background, offering a line of recession to the surging wave of figures which, from now on, are no longer to be distinguished as the representatives of "civilization" surrounded by the elements of "nature," both being merged indistinguishably into the atmospheric vibration that envelops the entire picture. Just as Botticelli avoided localizing the scene in time and space by adding a variety of architectural elements and costumes, so Leonardo, even in the garments of his figures, avoided every historical allusion that might have located the scene in a definite time or place. Yet we feel the actual "presence" of the event far more compellingly than in Botticelli's *Adoration*; only it is not an historical but a natural event, and though it takes place in time, this time is not that of history but of natural phenomena. And this time being inseparable from space, both are manifested to our senses in the incontestable reality of the pictured phenomenon.

For this reason Leonardo, though he took a radically new approach to perspective, chided Botticelli for not abiding by its rules: "Sandro, you tell us not why some things appear lower than others. The eye, if placed between two parallel lines, will never see them from a distance great enough to make them coincide at a single point" (Cod. Atl. 120r). This quotation contains two distinct and, at first sight, contradictory statements. One declares that, without perspective, there is no explaining why in a picture things near at hand appear lower than things at a distance. The other says that perspective theory, according to which two parallel lines coincide at a distant point, fails to correspond with visual experience. But both are border-line cases. The first is the negation of perspective scale; the second is the integral application of perspective theory, which amounts to the abrogation of spatial vision. Now Botticelli's spatial representation invariably oscillates between these two extremes; he systematically avoids giving any illusion of depth and three-dimensional form. As against the taut perspective of the throne in the *Fortitude*, the river bank in the *Man with a Medal* and the shore in the *Birth of Venus*, we get such distinctly anti-perspective solutions as that of the *Primavera*. Reduced to planes or radically schematized in the lines of a theoretical perspective, space has no effective depth to it, just as the figures have no effective volume or mass; space and figures alike are mere images or symbols.

The *Primavera* was painted about 1478. At that time Botticelli and Leonardo were unquestionably the most advanced painters in Florence, and both were equally committed to the struggle against what might be called the enlightened traditionalism of Baldovinetti and the middling Tuscan prose of Ghirlandaio. These circumstances go far towards explaining the hidden message of the picture, which certainly overshoots the mark of the humanist program it ostensibly illustrates. Gombrich recently made a thorough study of that program (*Botticelli's Mythologies*, in the *Journal of the Warburg and Courtauld Institutes*, Vol. VIII, 1945) and definitely established several important points: (1) the classical source of the theme is a

PRIMAVERA (ALLEGORY OF SPRING), CA. 1478. (79¾ × 123½") UFFIZI, FLORENCE.

passage in Apuleius; (2) the picture is meant to represent Venus-Humanitas and (3) closely parallels a passage in Marsilio Ficino. Thus its dominant character is one of *ekphrasis*, i.e. it stems from the descriptions of real or imaginary pictures frequently met with in the classical authors. Far be it from us to belittle the significance of the fact that this picture, like the *Calumny of Apelles* later on, is not intended to be a direct representation but the free reconstitution of an ancient painting known to us only by the written description of it. Here we need not dwell on the literary character of the work, nor for that matter on the host of symbols and allusions it contains or even on the striking contrast between it and Leonardo's nearly contemporary *Adoration of the Magi*. The important thing for us to note is that the two men's quarrel over perspective may have been the pretext for the *Primavera*, which must have appeared at the time as Botticelli's manifesto against perspective as the structural principle of the picture.

Here again, as in his Uffizi *Adoration of the Magi*, the leading role falls to the most distant figure, the pivot on which the secondary figures hinge. Of the standard distribution of figures by means of perspective practically nothing remains. Instead, a new power of rhythmic continuity is set in motion around the central figure, axis and caesura of that rhythm. Like written poetry, like that of Poliziano and Lorenzo the Magnificent in particular, the composition develops in metre and rhyme; rather than groups, the figures form stanzas and alternate with all the cadenced melodiousness of a *canzone*. The metre is scanned in the background by the unequal sequence of parallel treetrunks, alternately broad and narrow, silhouetted against a luminous sky. This variation in scale so completely defies the laws of perspective that we begin to wonder whether Leonardo's objection ("Sandro, you tell us not why some things appear lower than others...") may not allude to this picture, or anyhow to this peculiar manner of locating images in a spatial continuum.

When we further note that the flowery clearing is viewed as an inclined plane fastened to the backdrop without any depth or recession, then we realize that the picture is actually conceived as a tapestry, a *tabula picta*; it is like the transcription of a mental image, absolutely two-dimensional, and was never intended to convey the illusion of depth. The figures, moreover, conform

to that depthlessness in every respect, being aligned rather than echeloned, and contained in a thin, undefined "slice" of space. Thus movement, lacking the space it needs to evolve in and deprived of every reference to definite action, is merely "fictive" movement. Take the group of the Three Graces: the movement of the bodies, faintly suggested by the tilt of the figures, would have meant nothing were it not re-echoed and amplified by the fluttering veils. This was a stock procedure of classical art, discussed by Alberti and used by Leonardo. Veils puffed out in full curves by the wind plant the figure solidly in space and link it up with nature.

But nature in the *Primavera* being a tissue of symbols, this link takes on new meaning. It connects the image of humanity aspiring to merge itself with nature (or rather to allegorize nature) and the image of nature tending to assume the shape of "humanitas." Nowhere is the influence of Agostino di Duccio so distinct as in the rhythms of this picture. The motion of these veils, as in Agostino's bas-reliefs, seems to be contained, if not entirely in the picture plane, at least in a strict minimum of depth. And again as in Agostino's reliefs, the swayings and windings of line tend to sublimate physical matter, to give it the imponderable substance of light. More precisely, line tends to *become* light instead of *receiving* light. Thanks to these linear rhythms, dictated by the transparency of the veils, figures attain an almost absolute value of diaphaneity. And line, by achieving its purest graphic quality, reveals itself as the ultimate determination of light—light as "intellectual" as that of Fra Angelico's San Marco frescos is "mystical," light detached, in accordance with neo-Platonic theory, from all matter.

For the first time figures are defined not by one line but by several, by a cluster of lines among which it is impossible to distinguish the true contour-line of a body. Leonardo too was aware that "the edges of objects are not linear" and that "line can suggest two things: that which it contains or that in which it is contained, in other words the body which it circumscribes or the atmosphere that limits the body" (Lionello Venturi, *La critica d'arte e Leonardo da Vinci*, Bologna 1919, p. 167). Even in his drawings lines cluster together to such an extent that there is no telling which line exactly delimits the contour of a body. But Leonardo regarded nature as the physical movement of luminous and atmospheric masses, so that a profusion of lines was needed to render the modifications of form in the ceaseless variations of atmosphere. Botticelli, on the other hand, denied or ignored the physical existence both of bodies and space, which he regarded as mere images. And since an image is highly variable both in its contours and meanings, it cannot be defined by a single brushstroke. Even a line apparently so continuous and unique as that delineating the figure of Mercury, on the left side of the *Primavera*, neither forms the "limit of a body" nor models volumes with anything like the firmness of,

MARS AND VENUS, CA. 1475. (27½×68″)
REPRODUCED BY COURTESY OF THE TRUSTEES, NATIONAL GALLERY, LONDON.

for example, Pollaiolo's line; it glides like a fluid, suggesting the throb of contact between the diaphanous zone of light and the opaque zone of darkness.

But this is not all. Take two such works as *Pallas and the Centaur* (Uffizi) and *Mars and Venus* (National Gallery, London), painted shortly before the *Primavera*. The figure of Pallas Athena obviously prefigures the rhythmic movement treated on a grander scale in the Three Graces, while in the recumbent figure of Mars we find the same fluid continuity of contour as in that of Mercury. But in these earlier works—whose content and classical prototypes have been investigated by Gombrich—forms are firmer and better defined. Botticelli recorded the image of these divinities with the utmost clarity of definition, as if doing his best to second Marsilio Ficino's efforts to rehabilitate the gods of classical mythology. Allegory is handled much more simply than in the *Primavera*, and given the concrete, three-dimensional setting that is completely lacking in the latter picture, in which spatial recession was rejected in the interests of rhythm.

The head of the central figure of the *Primavera* stands out against the dark screen of a thicket—the same device we noted in the *Portrait of Ginevra Benci*, which seems to confirm the contacts between Botticelli and Leonardo at this critical juncture of Florentine culture. But the function of filtering and diffusing light which was assigned to the thick foliage of the juniper tree in Leonardo's portrait is, in the *Primavera*, exactly inverted. Here the thicket forms a dark halo around the figure, whose contours it follows; then it thins out and its leaves and branches are flatly silhouetted against the distant patch of sky. The transition from the light-filled face to the dark screen of the thicket is made by a headdress of transparent veils, which shade off rapidly from extreme diaphaneity to extreme opacity, from the most "spiritual" to the most "material" level. If we have here—as I believe we do—a deliberate allusion to Leonardo's *Portrait of Ginevra Benci*, then we may actually be said to witness Botticelli's efforts to intellectualize the results of one of Leonardo's first attempts to experiment with the data of reality. The ideological situation of the two men then stood as follows: the old unity of nature and history had been sundered; but whereas Leonardo boldly set up nature against history, Botticelli proceeded to transpose both into the purely intellectual value of poetry and attempted an interpretation of nature above and beyond considerations of knowledge, and an interpretation of history above and beyond moral considerations.

But if nothing concrete is represented in the picture, are we to conclude that in the painter's eyes all action is pointless? And if the figures move in a sphere devoid of positive moral interests, have moral values become meaningless? Had the ideal of the active life, extolled so highly only a few decades earlier by Coluccio Salutati and Leonardo Bruni, already fallen low in men's estimation? Certainly not, as is abundantly proved not only by the writings of the philosophers and literati, the policies of Lorenzo the Magnificent and the sermons of Savonarola, but even by Botticelli's painting. Only now that ideal of action was regarded subjectively; it was applied by Botticelli not to the figures depicted, but to himself, to his inspiration, to the *furor* of his inspiration. For Leonardo this *furor* sprang simultaneously from the artist's soul and from the natural world, and thus found expression equally well in the convulsive movement of figures and in the cosmic fury of natural phenomena. In Botticelli's painting, however, the almost feverish anxiety and the inner movement of figures were necessarily accompanied by a contemplative condition, a tremulous solitude, an aloofness from effective action. What mattered was "inward" action, the struggle between the subtle spirit and stolid matter, between light and darkness.

Are we therefore to conclude that the *Primavera* is, in the last analysis, a religious picture? And that Botticelli, at the far end of the 15th century, had reverted to the ascetic exercises of Fra Angelico? The parallel is legitimate enough, except that in Botticelli we find no counterpart to Angelico's resolute didacticism and politico-religious creed. It was in these very years, significantly enough, that we first meet with the legend of Beato Angelico, the "blessed," the "angelic" mystic, painting ineffable visions in a more or less permanent state of ecstatic piety. We are indebted for this legend to the complete inability of Botticelli's generation to discern the true historical background of Angelico's art, i.e. the intensely positive character of his religious outlook, still motivated by the essentially medieval desire to explain the world and creation.

It is instructive in this connection to compare the Uffizi *Adoration of the Magi* with the *Primavera*. The first has a religious, the second a profane subject. Yet the first stands in relation to the second exactly as Angelico's "naturalistic" works (e.g. the *Descent from the Cross*) stand in relation to such "ecstatic" works as the San Marco frescos. While not explicitly religious, the *Primavera* is the very expression of intellectual ecstasy—not the ecstasy of mere contemplation but of fervid inward activity. Thereupon the plurality or polyvalence of meanings contained in the picture is no longer simply a literary play of allegories; it is proof, on the contrary, that Botticelli had at last conferred on the image the same total, universal character that Piero della Francesca had conferred on form.

Botticelli's indictment of the prosaic naturalism and concrete social bias of Ghirlandaio's art is contained in the important fresco of *St Augustine in his Study*, painted in 1480 close by Ghirlandaio's *St Jerome*, in the Ognissanti church in Florence. Now that the Church had revised its hostile attitude towards the humanists, St Augustine and St Jerome were considered as

SIC AVGVSTINVS SACRIS SE TRADIDIT VT NON
MVTATVM SIBI ADHVC SENSERIT ESSE LOCVM

ST AUGUSTINE IN HIS STUDY, 1480.
(79½ × 63¾″) FRESCO, OGNISSANTI CHURCH, FLORENCE.

"ancients," not simply as saints and fathers of the Church, but philosophers and scholars. There is a sharp ideological difference between the two frescos: St Jerome is shown as the scholar who established the text of the Scriptures, St Augustine as the thinker who redeemed classical philosophy, notably that of Plato, and "converted" it to Christianity.

St Jerome then symbolizes the necessity of respecting the Scriptures to the letter, and Ghirlandaio represented him as a diligent philologist amid the instruments of his labors (candle, spectacles, scissors). St Augustine, on the other hand, stands for the necessity of apprehending the spirit of the Scriptures, and Botticelli accordingly represented him as an inspired visionary amid the symbols of that humanist culture whose intimate tie with Christianity Renaissance man set so much store by (astrolabe, book of Pythagorean theorems, etc.). But what was new here, and destined to have far-reaching repercussions, was Botticelli's transformation of the "famous man," venerated for the grandeur of his actions, into the "hero," the incarnation of an idea. Hence the set features of the face and the structural solidity, not to say monumentality, of the figure, which plays up the contrast with the rather cramped architecture and the foreshortening from below. In the mind of the artist, now that the problem of visualizing nature had been settled in the *Primavera*, the religious problem was coming to a head in the contradiction between the historical character of the Christian doctrine on the one hand and the Christian's ascetic impulse and feverish anticipation of grace on the other.

The *Transfiguration* (Pallavicini Collection, Rome), painted about the same time as *St Augustine in his Study*, reflects the same contradiction but shows the artist inclining towards asceticism. Represented on the side panels are *St Augustine* and *St Jerome*, symbolizing the two paths of election, equally indispensable. But these two figures, cramped in deeply recessed cubicles, have the effect of throwing the central scene—directly inspired by Angelico's San Marco frescos—into strong relief and bringing it on to the picture surface. Christ (flanked by Moses and St John the Baptist, the first and last prophets of the revelation) is a radiant source of light, while a sharp separation, barely feasible in this exiguous space, is made between the three holy men and the cringing apostles. No trace of historical narrative remains, nor even of the Gospel miracle; this is the direct, exalted figuration of dogma. There is no perspective justification for the radically contorted foreshortening of the three apostles' figures, which might have been lifted straight from the work of some late Trecento painter. Line and light assume symbolic functions, and these foreshortenings and this maze of lines in tension is meant to express the impotence of man before the blinding revelation of the divine, and man's spasmodic efforts to rise from the heavy earth to which his body is chained. The image is the symbolic and tangible form of dogma; from the poetic theme Botticelli had now passed on to the theme of doctrine and faith, moving steadily away from nature which he regarded now as inept to embody or explain the transcendental truth of God.

With the *Transfiguration*, in addition to the *Trinity* (Lord Lee of Fareham Collection, Richmond Park), the first illustrations of Dante and, above all, the Sistine frescos, Botticelli broke away for good from nature considered as the domain and secret explanation of all allegory. From now on he cultivated a new type of allegory, entirely conceptual, which finally coincided with that indestructible unity of letter and spirit which we call symbol.

It may seem strange that at this stage Botticelli should have embarked on such a work as the Sistine frescos, a grand cycle of paintings manifestly intended to demonstrate the historical basis of the Christian religion. Recent investigation has shown that the Sistine Chapel was meant to stand as the monument of the new lease of life won by the Roman Church after the healing of the Schism, as the tangible demonstration of the historical foundation of the Church and the continuity between the Old and New Testaments. It was "the ark of salvation, the shrine of Moses, the sanctuary in which the Lord reigns eternal." The dimensions of the Chapel were made to correspond with those of the Temple of Solomon in so far as they can be deduced from Scripture; it was fortified externally as being the strong-hold of the Faith; and in the original 15th-century decorations "the main theme was the salvation of mankind, first through the miraculous survival of Noah's ark in the deluge, then through the covenant with Moses, consecrated by the building of the Temple of Solomon, and finally through the Redemption and the handing over of the keys to St Peter" (E. Battisti, *Atti del Congresso Rinascimento ed Antico*, Florence 1956).

Botticelli was summoned to Rome to decorate the Sistine Chapel in 1481, together with Cosimo Rosselli, Domenico Ghirlandaio and Perugino, and we may take it for granted that he, probably more than the others, had a voice in the planning of the work. His contribution consists of three frescos: *The Purification of the Leper and the Temptation of Christ, Scenes from the Life of Moses, The Punishment of Korah, Dathan and Abiram*. None can be said to have any unity of action or to be conceived and composed as befits historical narrative; all, on the other hand, convey a doctrinal and symbolic message. In the first, for example, two different themes are purposely combined: to the arch-tempter Christ replies with the words from Deutoronomy and the Book of Psalms; the leper healed, He bids him seek out a priest and offer up a sacrifice, *"quod praecepit Moyses."* Thus the painter chose to illustrate those particular passages of the Gospel story which prove Christ's solemn acknowledgment of the Mosaic law.

The second fresco illustrates episodes in the life of Moses: slaying an Egyptian, taking flight, defending Jethro's daughters, kneeling before the apparition of God in the burning bush, leading the Israelites out of Egypt. Moses here prefigures Christ; just as Moses, at the Lord's bidding, redeemed the Israelites from servitude and led them home, so Christ, sent by the Father, redeemed humanity from the Original Sin and led it back to the Kingdom of God. This is the classical theme of parallel lives, exemplified in Plutarch.

In the third fresco Korah, Dathan and Abiram, having rebelled against the laws, are banished from the community and destroyed by the divine wrath. This was a stringent admonition to heretics and abettors of schisms: God will always confirm, and with righteous anger, the judgments pronounced by the one who acts in His name and represents Him on earth. But this is a rebellion not only against the laws of Moses, but also against the Roman laws; hence, in the center background, the Arch of Constantine, the emperor who in the 4th century recognized the legitimacy of Christianity and adopted it as the official religion of the Roman Empire.

In view of the ideology behind these frescos, it was only natural for the artist to avoid unified narrative composition and—after the manner of medieval painters—to group several episodes and the same figures several times in the same scene. It was only natural for him to avoid a strict application of perspective and to render space differently according to the different episodes represented. The first fresco, for example, is made up of five distinct episodes: the first temptation on a beetling crag at the right, above a shining city symbolizing earthly riches; the second temptation on the pinnacle of the temple; the third temptation on the mountain at the left; then Christ comes down from the mountain and bids the leper accomplish the sacrifice; lastly, in the center foreground, the

Bo. 20

THE PURIFICATION OF THE LEPER AND THE TEMPTATION OF CHRIST, 1481-1482.
(11 FT. 4 IN. × 18 FT. 2 IN.) FRESCO, SISTINE CHAPEL, VATICAN.

leper presents himself to the priest for purification. Now although the picture space is partitioned according to the episodes, the connection between them is neither a narrative nor a demonstrative one. The lay-out is almost exactly symmetrical: in the center the temple façade serves as a visual link between the temptation and the purification; on either side, like movable sets, a mountain slope; in the distance, right and left, two cities bathed in golden light. Filing in from each side, the two figure groups meet in the persons of the leper and the priest.

SCENES FROM THE LIFE OF MOSES, 1481-1482.
(11 FT. 5 IN. × 18 FT. 3 IN.) FRESCO, SISTINE CHAPEL, VATICAN.

The fresco showing *Scenes from the Life of Moses,* on the other hand, is laid out in terms of oblique planes which serve as platforms for the various episodes. The crowd of Israelites setting out for the promised land fills up the left side of the picture, while up to the bleak horizon the right is practically empty. The bend in the path pursued by Moses on the right emphasizes the eccentricity of the composition. In the foreground Moses is pouring water into the trough for the sheep tended by Jethro's daughters; behind the well is Moses again,

85

THE PURIFICATION OF THE LEPER AND THE TEMPTATION OF CHRIST, 1481-1482.
DETAIL: THE LEPER PRESENTING HIMSELF TO THE PRIEST.
FRESCO, SISTINE CHAPEL, VATICAN.

driving away the insolent shepherds. These two episodes immediately succeed each other in time; to stress the fact, the painter sets them against a common background: the dark hillock with a clump of trees. With their long trunks, these trees also connect the foreground episodes with those beyond: Moses taking off his shoes and receiving the divine revelation.

THE PURIFICATION OF THE LEPER AND THE TEMPTATION OF CHRIST, 1481-1482.
DETAIL: THE LEPER PRESENTING HIMSELF TO THE PRIEST.
FRESCO, SISTINE CHAPEL, VATICAN.

On the right stands a classical edifice in slanting perspective; this too is a "stage set" whose dual function is to connect the two successive episodes of Moses slaying the Egyptian and taking flight and, by pointing towards the horizon, to suggest the precipitation of Moses' fleeting figure and the distance that lies before him. The structure of the fresco reposes on the verticals of pillars and treetrunks and on the sinuous contours

THE PURIFICATION OF THE LEPER AND THE TEMPTATION OF CHRIST, 1481-1482. DETAIL OF THE LANDSCAPE. FRESCO, SISTINE CHAPEL, VATICAN.

Bo. 24

THE PURIFICATION OF THE LEPER AND THE TEMPTATION OF CHRIST, 1481-1482.
DETAIL: THE FIRST TEMPTATION. FRESCO, SISTINE CHAPEL, VATICAN.

of the hillocks, and their rhythm is the rhythm of the figures
erect but flexed by the slow taut curves of the foreground.

The violent action of the third fresco is expressed by the
concentration of movement in turbulent figure groups separated
by empty spaces. Syncopated and spasmodic, the rhythm stirs
to life unawares in the first group on the left, and that violent
exordium reverberates out to the horizon-line along the façade

SCENES FROM THE LIFE OF MOSES, 1481-1482. DETAIL OF THE EXODUS.
FRESCO, SISTINE CHAPEL, VATICAN.

of a sharply foreshortened building. Image of the laws, the
Arch of Constantine looks impassibly down on the final episode,
the punishment of the rebels, while on the right a ruined

SCENES FROM THE LIFE OF MOSES, 1481-1482. DETAIL OF JETHRO'S DAUGHTERS.
FRESCO, SISTINE CHAPEL, VATICAN.

portico forms the background of the group of indignant Israelites. The point to be made is that every element in the background of the three frescos corresponds to a particular episode.

Space is modulated according to the rhythm and tempo of each episode—not according to the narrative, for properly speaking there is no narrative. Each episode is the figurative expression of an idea, whose power of persuasion is proportionate to the persuasive power of the figures. And this power is stepped up or down according to the function of the figure in the context. Moses slaying the Egyptian, for instance, is a figure slashed in with swift strokes of the brush; the daughters of Jethro sway beside the well with a slow, willowy rhythm; the rebellious Korah, Dathan and Abiram are convulsive, vehement, frenzied figures. At every turn we find a manner of lingering over figures or dashing them off in a flash which has no precedent in painting, but which very possibly stemmed from a careful reading of Dante and a keen appreciation of his imagery. Indeed the drawings for the *Divine Comedy* prove how deeply Botticelli's style—though not his thematic material—was influenced by the study of Dante.

But if Botticelli was so adept at grasping the purely mental quality of Dante's images, how account for the fact that precisely in these frescos figures acquire a new plenitude of form, and that the artist takes an almost sensual delight in lingering over their beauty? Note that in each painting there are vivid, spontaneous, realistic touches, side by side with allegorical intentions, allusions to doctrine, and extreme refinements of beauty in the rhythm of lines, in the skillful interlinking of complicated figure groups, in the alternation of groups in movement and at rest, in the choice and harmony of colors, in the moderate yet sensitive use of gold as the symbol of light. Note the picture space which, though it owes little to empirical experience, nevertheless retains all the beauty and fascination of natural landscapes; and which not only stretches away before our eyes as through an open window, but invites us towards the light of far horizons and the glades of pleasant woodlands.

Deliberately, it seems, the painter offers those who contemplate his work—in this case pilgrims to Rome from all countries and classes of society—several keys to its meaning. Whoever sees with eyes alone, whoever sticks to the letter or lacks the science to understand "the doctrine concealed beneath the veil of strange verses" (Dante, *Inferno*, Canto IX), will go no further than the painted story. Whoever sees with the mind's eye and works back from effect to cause, from form to substance, will discover the ideological content and the allegorical meaning. But whoever lives the pure life of the intellect and burns with the desire to know the supreme good will grasp the spirit of these works, perceive the lofty beauty of them, and comprehend not only their metaphorical but their metaphysical significance. Based on a whole train of allusions and implications, this latitude of interpretation is one of the fundamental canons, scholastic in origin, of Dante's poetic imagery (cf. J. von Schlosser, *Die Kunstliteratur*, Vienna 1924, p. 70), and from now on it became one of the fundamentals of Botticelli's pictorial imagery.

A rash conclusion? I think not, for from this time on Botticelli was to all intents and purposes preoccupied with defining types of beauty which, while losing none of their intellectual value, made an immediate appeal; with setting up rhythms as musical, as "cantabile" as possible; with presenting human figures which, while remaining purely spiritual, are also amiable. Suffice it to mention the famous tondo known as the *Madonna of the Magnificat* (Uffizi), painted about 1483. Compared with the finesse of style and boldness of composition displayed by Botticelli elsewhere, this work has features that might almost seem trite. Compared with the London tondo of the *Adoration of the Magi*, it comes as a distinct surprise, with its entire composition regulated by the circular shape of the panel and its facile play of curves pressing the figures into the center.

THE MADONNA OF THE MAGNIFICAT, CA. 1483. (DIAMETER: 45¼″)
UFFIZI, FLORENCE.

The Virgin, like the daughters of Jethro, is an alluring young
woman with full red lips; the Child is as adorable as can be;
the angels are comely adolescents. But beneath these surface

◄ THE MADONNA OF THE MAGNIFICAT (DETAIL), CA. 1483. UFFIZI, FLORENCE.

charms is a hidden inner beauty. Our awareness of it grows as we realize that this gracious network of lines converges not towards a central point, but towards the scintillating S-shaped river in the background; and that the peripheral fulcrum of the composition is formed by the meeting of the Virgin's and angel's hands on the lower left. The rhythm then is not so cadenced and "decorative" as at first it seems; on the contrary, it is so subtle and intricate that as we follow it we lose sight of the physical beauty of the figures and, in spite of ourselves, are swept up in a music of movement whose harmony is that of the celestial spheres.

But coming back to the Sistine frescos. Having seen the diversity of meanings and interpretations to which they lend themselves, extending from the outward form that pleases the eye of all to the doctrinal message intended for the many and the lofty spiritual satisfactions reserved for the few, we may ask ourselves whether this complex type of propaganda was really suited to the purposes of the Church. Perugino's *Christ giving the Keys to St Peter*, painted on a neighboring wall of the Sistine Chapel, is the very opposite of Botticelli's frescos. Its unity of time and place is absolute; only a single episode is dealt with; its symmetry and perspective are mathematically perfect. The scene is scaled down uniformly as the eye travels towards the horizon; dark strips of marble flooring indicate perspective projection and on this clean-cut plane figures stand out sharply and solidly, with polished colors and measured monumentality. True and clear, the formal geometry exactly conveys the truth and clarity of the religious message. Here no ambiguity is possible and Perugino's fresco, straightforward and perfectly univalent, proclaims a single truth in terms equally intelligible to all beholders. The high philosophy of pictorial form expounded by Piero della Francesca has ripened into the official expression of Catholic doctrine.

Between such widely different approaches, one proposing to initiate the masses into the culture of an élite, the other to demonstrate simpler truths clear to all, the Church never hesitated and of course chose the second. And the artist, soon to appear, who best succeeded in combining a universal appeal with the universal truths of Christianity and classicism, the painter equally popular with the masses and the élite, was by the very nature of things a disciple of Perugino: Raphael. Botticelli's frescos are probably greater works than any by Perugino, but it was the latter, not Botticelli, who left his mark on the art then being promoted by the Church.

After less than two years in Rome, Botticelli returned to Florence for good in 1482 and from then on his painting increasingly reflected the political and religious vicissitudes of his native city. The *Birth of Venus,* an allegorical theme closely connected with that of the *Primavera,* marked a momentary return to the neo-Platonic inspiration of earlier days. The sober, incisive linework, the thin, transparent colors and the starkness of ornamental detail come like a renewed declaration of the spiritual essence and naked truthfulness of Tuscan drawing. It is known to have been directly inspired by a passage in Poliziano's poem *La Giostra,* which in turn goes back to classical sources; but this is not enough to explain the inner meaning of the picture. It is interesting to note that, through the *ekphrasis* of Poliziano, Botticelli deliberately reverts to the theme of Venus Anadyomene, subject of a lost painting by Apelles, the painter traditionally regarded as the supreme master of line and the tutelary god of Tuscan artists (Fra Angelico's epitaph contains the words *"velut alter Apelles"*). Notwithstanding this reference to the supreme classical ideal, the typological analysis made by Gombrich has shown that the compositional scheme derives directly from the traditional lay-out of the Baptism of Christ.

Nor is this simply an instance of unwitting *contaminatio*. On the contrary, Botticelli's Venus corresponds to Ficino's Venus-Humanitas, just as her birth from the foaming waters of the sea corresponds to the rebirth of the human soul in the ablutionary waters of baptism.

We are hardly justified in drawing any doctrinal conclusions from this correspondence, but it nevertheless goes to show the essentially spiritual—and not sensual—significance of the picture. Angelico too insisted on the necessity of viewing nature without sensuality if the purity of its God-created forms is

THE BIRTH OF VENUS, CA. 1485. (68¾ × 109¾")
UFFIZI, FLORENCE.

to be appreciated. But for Botticelli it was an intellectual virtue that triumphed over sensuality, and this lovely naked woman rising from the waves, her physical charms sublimated in the diaphaneity of her forms and the purity of her lines, is a challenge —an intellectual challenge—to sensuality. As for the landscape, Francastel has rightly observed that it is only a backdrop, devoid of depth. The whitecaps are merely circumflex accents against the pale blue of the water; rather than waves these are the abstract symbols of waves, serving to show that the blasts of the zephyrs have stirred up a choppy sea. But this is not a deliberately chosen symbol; it is born, almost spontaneously, of the systematic reduction of natural appearances to their most immaterial and intellectual element: line. The *Primavera* was an intricate tissue of allusions and possible meanings; the extreme sharpness of definition characterizing the *Birth of Venus* conveys its symbolism unequivocally. In all probability its hidden meaning is to be sought for in the presence, visible or invisible, of the four elements: the boundless expanse of water; the good earth, as fecund as the sea is barren; the life-giving air; the fire or spirit whose presence is implied by the flame-like locks of hair and the wind-blown mantle. Humanity is born to civilization, and coming out of nowhere lands on the shores of nature, who welcomes and clothes it. Though certainly subsequent to it (both however painted for Lorenzo di Pierfrancesco de' Medici, Marsilio Ficino's favorite disciple—not to be confused with Lorenzo the Magnificent), the *Birth of Venus* is like the antecedent of the *Primavera*; it emphasizes the first term (Venus, mother of creation) of the binomial Venus-Humanitas, while the *Primavera* emphasized the second (Humanitas, or civilization and culture).

The theme of Venus-Humanitas reappears in the two frescos painted in 1486 for the marriage of Giovanna degli Albizzi and Lorenzo Tornabuoni. The allegorical theme is quite simple:

LORENZO TORNABUONI AND THE LIBERAL ARTS, 1486. (83¼×111½")
FRESCO. LOUVRE, PARIS.

in one fresco Venus introduces Giovanna to the Three Graces, while in the other she leads Lorenzo into the presence of the Liberal Arts. But what is new is the poetic aura that hangs over these delicate visions, a charm that comes straight from the Trecento, from the *dolce stil novo* and Petrarch. Never before in painting had the rhythm of line and composition come so close

GIOVANNA DEGLI ALBIZZI AND THE CARDINAL VIRTUES, 1486. (83¼ × 111½″)
FRESCO. LOUVRE, PARIS.

to the broken yet melodious cadence of the *canzone*; even the
colors are harmonized in subtle consonances and dissonances
that have no apparent connection with space and light. The
Graces, for example, stand weightless and virtually motionless,
and if their garments seem to float as if stirred by the breeze,
this is only because their nature is not earthly but ethereal.

LORENZO TORNABUONI AND THE LIBERAL ARTS, 1486. DETAIL:
LORENZO TORNABUONI. FRESCO, LOUVRE, PARIS.

GIOVANNA DEGLI ALBIZZI AND THE CARDINAL VIRTUES, 1486. DETAIL:
GIOVANNA DEGLI ALBIZZI. FRESCO. LOUVRE, PARIS.

PORTRAIT OF GIULIANO DE' MEDICI. (21¼ × 14¼")
KAISER FRIEDRICH MUSEUM, BERLIN.

The floating and subsiding of their garments is a movement beautiful in itself, not because it suggests the motion of their bodies or the breath of air, but because its rise and fall express the alternate and continuous movements of the soul; it is the abstract symbol of spirituality.

Then, just as line seems to free itself from the human figure and express movement independently, that abstract rhythm yields its secret meanings and meets the senses directly as an immediately perceptible entity. Out of its apparent abstraction line is seen to assume its constant value as the concrete, well-defined expression of form. And this is easily accounted for. Now that it has overcome every link with the tangible world, the image is no longer born of an immaterialization or spiritualization of the object, or of its aspiration towards a realm of pure ideas, since the idea itself, without losing any of its spirituality, can be manifested in tangible "signs." After all it is the idea that most clearly reveals the beauty constituting the specific character of the image. It is not too much to say that these two "visions" represent the extreme point of development, never to be surpassed, of Botticelli's neo-Platonism. Beyond this point no further aspiration or intellectual tension is conceivable —only the ardor and zeal of unquestioning faith. The acute religious crisis of Botticelli's maturity, authenticated beyond the shadow of a doubt, was certainly precipitated by Savonarola's fiery sermons, but it was also the inevitable conclusion of his own intellectual progress, as is amply proved by the fact that the first signs of its coming on preceded the crucial phase of the politico-religious struggle between Savonarola and the Medici.

The *Madonna with St John the Baptist and St John the Evangelist* (Berlin), datable to about 1485, is rigorously closed off by the fronds behind the figures, whose faces and bodies are drawn with an austerity verging on harshness. The composition is almost ritual in its compliance with traditional iconography.

The absolute immobility of the bodies is emphasized by the tension of the line, whose starkness and asperity suggest not physical movement but the inner tension of the soul. Botticelli, like Leonardo, relied on the movement of line to express the inner movements of people; but these movements, which for Leonardo were "mental accidentals," were for Botticelli the very substance of the spiritual life. For both men of course the inner life's history is written in the facial expression of figures; but while Leonardo showed its variety and mutability, Botticelli showed the continuity and constancy of its spiritual tension.

SALOME (FRAGMENT), CA. 1487. PREDELLA SCENE
FROM THE SAN BARNABA ALTARPIECE. UFFIZI, FLORENCE.

THE VISION OF ST AUGUSTINE (FRAGMENT), CA. 1487.
PREDELLA SCENE FROM THE SAN BARNABA ALTARPIECE. UFFIZI, FLORENCE.

Just as Ficino's mythological symbolism aimed at reconstituting the true image of the gods (Gombrich, *op. cit.* p. 56), so Botticelli now aimed at fixing the true image of the saints and picturing their heroic virtue as faithfully as possible. Frequently engraved at the time, prints of these paintings were published with pious versets appended to them and established a popular type of devotional image. The *Altarpiece of San Barnaba* (ca. 1487) seems to be an express attempt to standardize the large retable of that day, and to make the ritual of art into a true and proper liturgy. Three saints are lined up on each side of the Virgin, who is seated on a raised throne; two angels lift the flaps of the

THE MIRACLE OF ST ELIGIUS (FRAGMENT), 1488-1490. PREDELLA SCENE
FROM THE CORONATION OF THE VIRGIN ALTARPIECE. UFFIZI, FLORENCE.

canopy, while two others hold up nails and crown of thorns,
the symbols of the Passion. The entire composition is enclosed
in a broad archway, which may be taken to allude both to the
universality of the Church and, by its classical archivolt, to
the Roman background of the Church.

But for all its symbolism and ritual character, every detail
of the work vibrates with linear tension, while the predella
scenes are evocative, straightforward vignettes, as terse and
sententious as the versets of psalms, and as realistic and pungent
as popular sayings. It is this fusion of the doctrinal and the
ingenuous, of aristocratic speech and Tuscan plain-speaking,
this attitude more correctly styled *for* the people than *of* the
people, that constitutes the really Savonarolian phase of
Botticelli's painting. Was it not the Florentine people who, in
Savonarola's impassioned prophecies, were to lead humanity
along the way to moral redemption?

Hence the ritual severity of composition we find in the great *Coronation of the Virgin* (Uffizi), that celestial vision so concrete and immediate that we might almost reach up and touch it with the hand. It purports to demonstrate that the truth of dogma is a positive reality for those who, like these four saints, have attained a certain heroic toughness of moral fibre. Here again the predella scenes are vivid, sententious, crystal-clear. Firm now in his conviction that art's highest mission is religious apostleship, he rejects the polemics of old as being senseless, and in the very attitudes he had once contended against for ideological reasons he now finds proof of the perennial vitality of Florentine pictorial expression. Here, for example, in the predella panels of the *Annunciation* and *St Jerome* are unexpected echoes of Leonardo's Florentine paintings: the abbreviated

ST JOHN IN PATMOS (FRAGMENT), 1488-1490. PREDELLA SCENE
FROM THE CORONATION OF THE VIRGIN ALTARPIECE. UFFIZI, FLORENCE.

movements of figures, the fusion of light and perspective, the vibrant light and atmosphere of the landscape. The *St Augustine* panel is lit up by strong light coming in from the side, by *true* light, whose incidence casts well-marked shadows and which reduces the table-top on which the saint is writing to a sharp, luminous line and also foreshortens perspective distances. The construction of the *St Eligius* panel is pre-eminently pictorial, made up of vivid color contrasts.

The *Annunciation* (ca. 1488) formerly in the church of Santa Maria Maddalena dei Pazzi (now in the Uffizi) is reminiscent of Lippi in the tenuous half-light of the chamber, the perspective projection of the checkered flooring, the melting attitudes of figures. The position of the Virgin at the extreme edge of the picture, as if she were about to step outside the frame, comes straight from Donatello's *Annunciation* in the Cavalcanti Chapel at Santa Croce, as does something of the *contractio animi* and the religious tension. The angel is entirely absorbed in the simultaneous action of arresting its flight and bowing down, and its movements resound, as it were, in the slow curves of the swooning Virgin. No doubt but that this is one of Botticelli's most beautifully "modeled" works. Yet his modeling, ignoring chiaroscuro and volume relief, springs directly from the conjunction of light and movement. It consists of a rich complex of light effects—side-lighting, direct lighting, transparency, even diffusion. But the solidity of form which results—unusual with Botticelli—by no means produces a scene "after nature" or "from the life." What we have is the recording of an image in an infinite gradation of light values.

Therewith, after a long, tortuous, intellectual advance, Botticelli finally stood on the open threshold to which Leonardo had acceded at one bound; at last, that is, he felt space to be light and the movement of figures to be their ardent participation in the mobile substance of the cosmos. But for a painter who had never regarded his art as a vehicle of knowledge or a product of reality, what were the consequences of his intuitive realization that the image is not a transcending of the object but is of itself the very form and thing of reality in all its concreteness and plenitude? In falling back on the world and joining forces with the will to action, Botticelli's spiritual yearnings not unnaturally found their principal outlet in a redoubled moral zeal, and though his exquisite sense of pictorial poetry never deserted him, his last works are moral, not to say moralistic, with a vengeance.

Having set himself a moral purpose he put all his resources to its service, displaying the full range of his technical knowledge and humanist culture in the *Calumny of Apelles* (ca. 1494). Once more, having proposed to reconstitute a lost work by Apelles, he proved his familiarity with the ancient texts and his insight into the allegorical significance of figures and colors. He laid out the scene in flawless perspective and distributed figures according to established canons, avoiding both crowding and isolation. He studied body movements and facial expressions one by one and delineated them with an extreme purity of design. This he plainly meant to make an exemplary work, perfect in execution and finish. Its austerity springs from the moral purpose he held before him, intent as he was on illustrating the hatefulness of lies, the frailty of human judgment, the beauty of truth.

The architectural background is minutely delineated down to the last detail of the allegorical statues and bas-reliefs decorating the dado, frieze and coffered ceiling. Here we recognize all the signs of a picture painted for the benefit of the "visitor," on his imaginary pilgrimage, come to admire the marvels of

PAGES 114-115:
THE CALUMNY OF APELLES (DETAILS), CA. 1494. UFFIZI, FLORENCE.

114

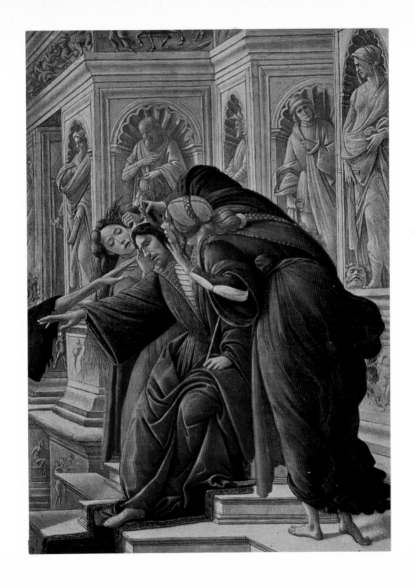

THE CALUMNY OF APELLES, CA. 1494. (24⅜ × 35¾")
UFFIZI, FLORENCE.

antiquity—the very theme of Dante's *Divine Comedy* and, in Botticelli's time, of Francesco Colonna's famous *Dream of Polyphile*. But then, as the "visitor" contemplates the splendor of antique forms and the wisdom of the moral examples manifested in them, the motionless scene all at once starts to life and something terrible and mysterious takes place. Only later does the pilgrim understand that this event, which strikes fear into the heart and which is endlessly repeated, has an allegorical and moral significance and that the actors of the drama are the personification of ideas. Antiquity then is more than a definite epoch of history; it is the remote domain of

THE DERELITTA, CA. 1490. (18 × 16½″) COLL. OF PRINCE PALLAVICINI, ROME.

THE LAST COMMUNION OF ST JEROME, CA. 1490. $(13\frac{3}{4} \times 10'')$
BY COURTESY OF THE METROPOLITAN MUSEUM OF ART, NEW YORK.

the ideas and motives behind human action. But herein lie the limits of ancient wisdom, for if the motives of human action remain always the same, if every event that occurs repeats a former event, if humanity has no history, then that wisdom cannot be said to produce any results or lead to final salvation; or rather, salvation is not attainable through the natural and moral philosophy of the ancients, but only through revelation and divine grace.

In the *Calumny*, whether consciously or not, Botticelli revealed these limits of ancient wisdom. For we may note that the rhythm of the line is not determined by stylistic reasons alone. Emphasizing the rigidity of the perspective and the hieratic formality of the architecture, movement starts off in the feet of the victim, rises in an unbroken crescendo towards the throne of the ill-counselled judge and from there, pivoting on the slewed form of the last figure on the right, returns along the judge's outstretched arm to its point of departure. Just as this movement endlessly recurs, so the violence and fury of the episode depicted will in this world endlessly recur, today, tomorrow, forever.

This is confirmed by the *Derelitta* or *Outcast* (Pallavicini Collection, Rome). Mention has been made in an earlier page of the most plausible interpretation of this picture: *Virtus* divorced from *Sapientia*. This theme is undoubtedly related to that of a drawing representing *The Faithless and the Descent of the Holy Ghost* (Darmstadt). The closed door signifies the exclusion of the soul from the place of beatitude. The cold wall of unrelieved stone is impenetrable, while the inviting perspective of the passageway only leads to the locked door topped with sharp spikes. These symbols re-echo those of the *Calumny* and allude to the divorce and incompatibility of the two doctrines—the futility of virtue deprived of supreme wisdom, i.e. of divine revelation.

PIETÀ, 1500. (42×28″) MUSEO POLDI-PEZZOLI, MILAN.

If this interpretation is exact and such works as the *Calumny* and the *Derelitta* are really to be regarded as a belated and sorrowful condemnation of that humanist thought which even then at Rome was falling in line with Christian thought, then we should expect to find a parallel set of roughly contemporary pictures demonstrating the artist's intensified religious zeal.

PAGES 122-123:
PIETÀ (DETAILS), 1500. MUSEO POLDI-PEZZOLI, MILAN.

PIETÀ, 1500. (55 × 81½") ALTE PINAKOTHEK, MUNICH.

And these we find indeed in the Hanover *Annunciation*, the *Last Communion of St Jerome* (New York), the Milan and Munich *Pietàs* and the great London *Nativity*, Botticelli's last dated work (1500). The extreme refinement of delineation and finish which we noted in the *Calumny of Apelles* was fully justified so long as the painter was expounding a moral truth; it became superfluous when he turned to illustrating the mysteries of the faith. Here discourses and dialectical argumentation are out of place; he can only attain his end by direct communication, pronounced in a flash.

In the Hanover *Annunciation* we find an additional figure, a woman kneeling in the foreground, much smaller than the more distant Virgin and angel; this then is a reversal of perspective relationship. The tones of their garments form a purely coloristic link between the luminous figure of the angel and the dark figure of the Virgin. What we have here is not the representation of an actual event or even a mystical vision; this is the miraculous revelation of a sacred mystery in the prayers of the devout. The image is swiftly, cursorily conjured up. Line circumscribes the color zones, marking the dark form of the leaning Virgin and the luminous counterpoise of the angel. Thus it is the intensity of the line that lifts the "timbre" of the colors to its highest pitch.

The *Pietà* in the Poldi-Pezzoli Museum, Milan, is the very opposite of the *Calumny*. Its moral allegory requires images as distinct as the ideas they personify, for the truth of faith is one and indivisible. Here indeed the image is unique, even though it is composed of several figures; the theme too is unique, though it comprises a range of thought running from the bare fact (personified by the limp body of Christ) to the symbol (represented by the crown of thorns and the nails).

PIETÀ (DETAIL), 1500. ALTE PINAKOTHEK, MUNICH. ▶

THE CRUCIFIXION, AFTER 1500. (28¾ × 20″)
FOGG ART MUSEUM, CAMBRIDGE (MASS.).

Unique too is the pathos expressed in the lines of force, rising in contrasting crescendos within the unity of the figure group, whose taut, articulate interplay of curves and angles is reminiscent of Gothic architecture. At the base of this pyramid of figures, perspectively framed in the entrance to the sepulchre, lie the full, crisp folds of the Virgin's mantle. Christ's body stands out in sharp angles against the shroud, whose broad curve is repeated, but inverted like a sustaining arch, in the full curve of the Magdalen's cloak. The overlapping arms, hanging vertically, of the Virgin and St John carry up the eye in syncopated rhythm towards the intensely emotional juxtaposition of heads. Beyond this no further gesture is possible, unless it be an ultimate catharsis, a fulfillment of the symbol. Only Michelangelo, years later, was capable of grasping the sense and scope of such a composition as this, which avoided both melodramatic crudeness and abstract ideas.

Vasari in his *Lives* noticeably overstresses Botticelli's decline and his apathetic "old age" (after all he was only 65 when he died). From this we may infer that by the time the 16th century had begun Botticelli was already regarded as an outmoded, old-fashioned artist. His last dated work is the London *Nativity*, painted in 1500, the very year in which Leonardo returned to Florence. Would it be arbitrary to assume that the old controversy between the two men now flared up again, sharpened by the deeply rooted religious convictions of the one and the proud scientific achievements of the other?

Whatever view we choose to take in the matter, one thing is certain: this *Nativity* stands out as one of the most archaistic and pietistic of Botticelli's works; it is intimately connected with the tense political and religious situation of that day, and is, at one and the same time, edifying and threatening. The unusual composition, with its hierarchical order of images, unfolds like a ritual in defiance of the laws of perspective. The whole scene is overdecorated, overembellished, overmusical in its evanescent, elusive rhythms; the bright colors and touches of gold are deliberately ingenuous, artisan-like, popular in their appeal. Nothing could be further removed from the molten, unified vision, the atmospheric *sfumato*, the vibrant light and broad design of Leonardo. When we remember the date of the picture and the achievements he had behind him at the time, Botticelli's attitude is seen to be more than archaistic, it is downright reactionary. And yet, even in this negative attitude, dead set against every recent advance in art, there lay a positive historical factor: the mature conviction that human emotions are not —as Leonardo would have it—reducible to natural movements because as often as not the essence of emotion lies not in nature but in religion or morals.

We know next to nothing of Botticelli's activities—certainly not very intense—in that first decade of the Cinquecento which saw the three geniuses of the century meet at Florence: Leonardo, Michelangelo and Raphael. But the themes and style of his works of that period leave no doubt as to their trend. Disregarding the new ideal of "monumentalism" sponsored by his rivals, Botticelli clung to his "Florentinism" of old, and in the Fogg *Crucifixion* he even reverted to a Giottesque motif in the background where we see angels driving devils out of Florence.

This reaction led him to paint several of his finest works, in particular the two panels illustrating the Roman legends of Virginia and Lucretia, which seem deliberately to substitute the cult of the small and precious for the regnant mania for the monumental. Through the imaginary classicism of their architecture, furthermore, these pictures set up the idea of classicism-plus-civilization against that of classicism-plus-nature, then on the rise, which must have seemed to Botticelli a grossly

THE NATIVITY, 1500. (42½ × 29½")
REPRODUCED BY COURTESY OF THE TRUSTEES, NATIONAL GALLERY, LONDON.

absurd and arbitrary confusion of values. Lastly, he intended to demonstrate that lofty dramatic action can only evolve within a web of great ideas. The architectural backgrounds of these panels, with their careful perspective, are reminiscent of Piero della Francesca, or rather of the relic cupboard of San Bernardino at Perugia.

The four oblong panels illustrating the life and miracles of St Zenobius—a work unique in Botticelli's output—carry us still further back in time, being reminiscent of the simple, clean-cut architecture of Fra Angelico's predella scenes. Now that Leonardo had moved on to aerial perspective in terms of atmospheric masses of varying density, Botticelli polemically reverted to the early experiments in perspective, to the early precepts for representing buildings, to the old conception of perspective planes laid out in clean-cut tracts of pure color.

THE TRAGEDY OF LUCRETIA, AFTER 1500. $(32\frac{3}{4} \times 70\frac{1}{4}'')$
THE ISABELLA STEWART GARDNER MUSEUM, BOSTON.

THE MIRACLES OF ST ZENOBIUS, AFTER 1500. (26 × 71½″)
GEMÄLDEGALERIE, DRESDEN.

But of course it was only a make-believe primitivism. While the composition, like that of Fra Angelico, may turn indeed on figure groups and intervals, with much of the same candor of expression and stiffness of movement, still the even tenor of the narrative is occasionally broken, without warning, by dramatic notes and accents of tragedy that Angelico had never known. How could he know them when for him miracle was the most natural manifestation of Providence, its normal manner of action in a natural world which itself is a miracle and from which the presence of God suffices to banish the dramatic element? For Botticelli, on the contrary, faith itself is instinct with drama and tragedy, for it is the relentless struggle of the spirit, which is light, translucency and tension, against matter, which is opaque and inert.

In this lies the real meaning of Botticelli's last meditations. Drama and tragedy are not only the stuff of history and rise in the souls of great men and heroes; they are also the stuff of the faith of the humble and the pure in heart. Savonarola by his

THE MIRACLES OF ST ZENOBIUS, AFTER 1500. (26½×59¼″)
BY COURTESY OF THE METROPOLITAN MUSEUM OF ART, NEW YORK.

death seemed to prove as much. This evolution of religious
thought towards an exalted, dramatic spiritualism was therefore
by no means confined to Botticelli's art; it had developed and
radiated from that fervent center of Quattrocento religious life,
the Dominican convent of San Marco in Florence, where the
Blessed Giovanni Dominici had preached at the beginning of
the century, where Fra Angelico had painted and prayed, where
Girolamo Savonarola had matured and conceived his great
designs of moral reform.

The efforts of St Antoninus, archbishop of Florence from
1446 to 1459, to indoctrinate the Florentine bourgeoisie and
the nobles of the Medici court with his own religious ideals,
and at the same time to effect a political alliance with the Curia
Romana, had to be written down as a failure. Several decades had
elapsed when his mild apostleship passed to Savonarola, who
preached a return to the simplicity of primitive Christianity

—but preached it with such inflammatory zeal that by the end of the century the monks of San Marco, loyal to him to a man, stood in open revolt against both the Medicis and the pope. And this was the drama of the future: the conflict between, on the one hand, a "spiritual" religion based exclusively on the direct connection of man's conscience with God and, on the other, a "natural" religion claiming to embrace in its universality all space and time and all nature and history.

It was not simply to sing the praises of the "good old days" that in some of his later works Botticelli reverted to the themes and methods of Fra Angelico. Botticelli's anti-naturalism was the necessary corollary of Angelico's religious naturalism; his undenominational religious outlook—an anxious personal quest of God—was the corollary of Angelico's religious convictions; his neo-Platonic aesthetic was the corollary of Angelico's

THE MIRACLES OF ST ZENOBIUS, AFTER 1500. (25 × 55″)
BY COURTESY OF THE TRUSTEES, NATIONAL GALLERY, LONDON.

133

THE MIRACLES OF ST ZENOBIUS (DETAIL), AFTER 1500.
BY COURTESY OF THE METROPOLITAN MUSEUM OF ART, NEW YORK.

Thomist aesthetic. The fact is that Botticelli and Angelico have a point in common that distinguished them from the other great masters of the 15th century, whose art was enlisted in the service of knowledge and man's experience of nature and

history. Both men possessed an aesthetical ideal, a vision of
perfection, of which they considered art to be not only the
expression but the practical, necessary realization. Both keenly
felt that art should be not only contemplation but action; and

CHRIST IN THE GARDEN OF OLIVES, CA. 1504. (20¾ × 13¾″)
CAPILLA REAL, GRANADA.

that as such it should influence human conduct, not simply by the representation of exemplary actions but by the artist's own conduct, which he should strive to make honorable and exemplary. Only thereby can he hope to transcend the limits of matter and the senses and attain that perfect communion with the Idea which—as Michelangelo spent his life demonstrating—is synonymous with spiritual "beauty" in contradistinction to natural "beauty."

SELECTED BIBLIOGRAPHY

INDEX OF NAMES

CONTENTS

# SELECTED BIBLIOGRAPHY

G. Vasari, *Vite de' più eccellenti Pittori, Scultori e Architettori*, edited by Milanesi, vol. III, Florence 1906. — C. Diehl, *Botticelli*, Paris 1906. — H. P. Horne, *Alessandro Filipepi, called Botticelli*, London 1908. — H. Gebhart, *Botticelli*, Berlin 1909. — A. Venturi, *Storia dell'Arte italiana*, vol. VII, 1st part, Milan 1910. — A. P. Oppé, *Sandro Botticelli*, London 1911. — J. Cartwright, *Sandro Botticelli*, London 1912. — W. Bode, *Sandro Botticelli*, Berlin 1921. — A. Schmarsow, *Sandro del Botticello*, Dresden 1923. — Y. Yashiro, *Sandro Botticelli*, London-Boston 1925. — A. Venturi, *Botticelli*, Rome 1925. — C. Gamba, *Botticelli*, Milan 1936. — L. Venturi, *Botticelli*, Paris 1937. — J. Mesnil, *Botticelli*, Paris 1938. — S. Bettini, *Botticelli*, Bergamo 1942 (with an exhaustive bibliography). — E. Gombrich, *Botticelli's Mythologies*, in *Journal of the Warburg and Courtauld Institutes*, vol. VIII, 1945. — C. L. Ragghianti, *Inizio di Leonardo*, in *La Critica d'Arte*, 1954. — A. Bertini, *Botticelli*, Milan 1954 (the drawings, with a bibliography). — A. Chastel, *Marsile Ficin et l'Art*, Geneva-Lille 1954. — E. Battisti, in *Atti del Congresso Rinascimento ed Antico*, Florence 1956 (forthcoming).

# INDEX OF NAMES

# CONTENTS

THIS VOLUME, THE NINETEENTH OF THE COLLECTION "THE TASTE OF OUR TIME", WAS PRODUCED BY THE TECHNICAL STAFF OF EDITIONS D'ART ALBERT SKIRA, FINISHED THE FIFTEENTH DAY OF FEBRUARY NINETEEN HUNDRED AND FIFTY-SEVEN.

TEXT AND ILLUSTRATIONS BY

COLOR STUDIO
AT IMPRIMERIES RÉUNIES S. A., LAUSANNE.

PLATES ENGRAVED BY GUEZELLE ET RENOUARD, PARIS.

*Photographs by Louis Laniepce, Paris (pages 104, 105), Claudio Emmer, Milan (pages 3, 6, 45, 57, 58, 59, 66, 72, 73, 84, 85, 86, 87, 88, 89, 90, 91, 92, 93, 96, 97, 108, 109, 110, 111, 114, 115, 120, 122, 123), Henry B. Beville, Washington (pages 46, 60, 63, 126, 130, 134), Walter Steinkopf, Berlin (pages 36, 53, 106), Zoltán Wegner, London (pages 10, 54, 75, 129, 135), Hans Hinz, Basel (pages 121, 125), and by courtesy of the Deutsche Fotothek, Dresden (page 131).*

PRINTED IN SWITZERLAND